Sweetheart & Mother Pillows
1917-1945

To My Wife

A darling little wife
Has made my dreams come true,
She blesses all my life.
Her name is only "You."

You are my partner sweet,
You share in all I do,
And make my joy complete
By simply being You !

CAMP CHAFFEE, ARK.

U.S.A.

NAVY

Mother O'Mine

I always think of mother
No matter where I roam
I always think of mother
Although I am far from home
Friends and many others
Sometimes prove untrue
But never does a mother
For her heart is always true

Patricia Cummings

Schiffer Publishing Ltd

4880 Lower Valley Road, Atglen, Pennsylvania 19310

Dedication

To every mother who has lost a son in battle,
and every soldier whose last word, as he lay dying, was "Mother"

Other Schiffer Books on Related Subjects:
Sweetheart Jewelry & Collectibles, 0-88740-834-6, $29.95
Antique Sweetheart Jewelry, 0-88740-902-4, $29.95
WWII Quilts, 978-0-7643-3451-1, $39.99

Copyright © 2011 by Patricia Cummings
Unless noted, all images are the property of the author.
Library of Congress Control Number: 2011935868

Designed by Mark David Bowyer
Type set in Snell BT / New Baskerville

ISBN: 978-0-7643-3917-2
Printed in China

Schiffer Books are available at special discounts for bulk purchases for sales promotions or premiums. Special editions, including personalized covers, corporate imprints, and excerpts can be created in large quantities for special needs. For more information contact the publisher:

Published by Schiffer Publishing Ltd.
4880 Lower Valley Road
Atglen, PA 19310
Phone: (610) 593-1777; Fax: (610) 593-2002
E-mail: Info@schifferbooks.com

For the largest selection of fine reference books on this and related subjects, please visit our website at:
www.schifferbooks.com
We are always looking for people to write books on new and related subjects. If you have an idea for a book, please contact us at **proposals@schifferbooks.com**

This book may be purchased from the publisher.
Include $5.00 for shipping.
Please try your bookstore first.
You may write for a free catalog.

In Europe, Schiffer books are distributed by
Bushwood Books
6 Marksbury Ave.
Kew Gardens
Surrey TW9 4JF England
Phone: 44 (0) 20 8392 8585; Fax: 44 (0) 20 8392 9876
E-mail: info@bushwoodbooks.co.uk
Website: www.bushwoodbooks.co.uk

Contents

Acknowledgments

· **James G. Cummings** provides encouragement, assistance, and his wonderful expertise with a camera. He has taken most of the photos that appear here and without him this book would not have been possible.

· **Lyell D. Henry** not only shared his extensive collection of pillow covers, gathered over a number of decades, he also granted permission to feature a charming parody that he wrote about the history of "Mother" pillows, previously published in the *Journal of Popular Culture*. As far as I know, he is the first writer to ever address this subject in print and I am the second one.

· **Louise G. Traunstein** provided a photo of herself and Cpl. Russell Traunstein, her "Sweetheart" husband, taken in 1944 before he shipped to Italy with the U.S. Armed Air Forces.

· **Alderic O. "Dick" Violette** is the only person I have ever met who served in both the Civilian Conservation Corps and World War II. He remembers all the words to the "Mother" song and delighted us by singing it to us. Thank you for sharing information about the Civilian Conservation Corps and thank you for your service to our country!

· **Martin A. Fischer (1924-1995)**, my mother's younger brother, sent her postcards and "V mail" from "Somewhere in England," "Somewhere in France," and "Somewhere in Germany." He was a member of a U.S. Army Field Artillery unit and fought in seven major World War II battles in Europe. Injured during the Battle of the Bulge, his patriotism and love of country were inspirational.

· **John M. Grace (1943-1996)**, my eldest brother, made me feel proud when he joined the Air Force. From Lackland Air Force Base, San Antonio, Texas, "Jack" sent me a heart-shaped piece of "Sweetheart" jewelry that says, "Sister," as well as a scarf with an Air Force logo.

· **Beth Davis**, a dear friend, found a very unique "Daughter" pillow, the only one I have seen while researching these kinds of textiles for years.

· **Laurette Koserowski**, editor of *The Quilter* magazine, published my first quilt article in 1999.

· **Patti Ives**, editor of *The Appliqué Society Newsletter*, who always has encouraging words for all of my writing projects.

Foreword

By Lyell D. Henry, Ph.D.

Well, it took a long while, but at last it has happened — someone else has joined me in tapping the rich mother lode of "Mother" pillow covers. Way back in 1971, when I was an administrator and a graduate student at the University of Iowa, I wrote the first research article ever done on this strangely neglected subject. Published in the *Journal of Popular Culture* (and reprinted in this book), my article purported to review what was then known about "Mother" pillow covers, laid out some lines of further inquiry, and tried to rally others to join the research effort. In spite of my blandishments and the subject's intrinsic appeal, however, there were never any takers — until this moment. Now, a full forty years after my initial foray, Patricia Cummings has blessed us with the splendid book that you hold in your hands.

In several major respects Patricia's work goes far beyond my article. For one thing, her book provides an abundance of close descriptive material and many dazzling images (thanks to the excellent camera work done by her husband, James Cummings). Alas, my pioneering piece could never be much more than a brief prolegomenon, aimed mostly at suggesting the subject's rich research potential. After all, there was then no body of research on "Mother" pillow covers for me to comment upon, and because I was busy working on a Ph.D. dissertation, I couldn't take time to do any research myself. My solution was to make up all the "facts" presented in my article, in the manner of H. L. Mencken's celebrated but bogus history of the bathtub.

Thus unburdened of the usual constraints on research, in a very brief space I concocted generalizations of breathtaking novelty, fabricated endnotes full of patent absurdities, and teased out deep cultural meanings from the (non-existent) pillow covers treated in my (imaginary) study. Although my piece was larded with many of the buzz words and conceits of academic prose, a faculty member of the English department pointed out that I could reach even greater clarity by adding a generous sprinkling of French, German, and Latin words. The finished article, I readily confess, tickled me inordinately, and working

on it also had provided two days of pleasant respite from the dreary chores of dissertation writing. After sending the article off to *The Journal of Popular Culture* with some feelings of trepidation, I was relieved and delighted to find that the editor of that great organ of learning had a sense of humor and rushed my phony article into print in that journal's very next issue.

I recount the above tale of academic malfeasance for the purpose of highlighting one more respect in which Patricia's work advances past mine: far from being the product of idle whimsy, her book is the record of a very serious and careful examination of hundreds of actual pillow covers. It's obvious that much diligence was needed to bring this book to fruition.

Patricia also brings to her book an expert's knowledge of textiles acquired from many years of study and many years, too, of making, collecting, and writing about quilts. Collectors and students of textiles have so far given no attention to souvenir pillow covers, but that may change now, thanks to her book; herein she provides useful information about the manufacture, handling, care, and conservation of the fabrics used in making souvenir pillow covers. Also likely to be of help to collectors are the estimated money values that Patricia provides for the nearly 250 pillow covers shown in the book. (Could a collection of "Mother" pillow covers today actually be like money in the bank? Doubtless prodded upward by eBay auctions, their values seem to have soared to great heights in recent years. In contrast, when I picked up pillow covers at flea markets and yard sales several decades ago I can't recall ever paying more than a few dollars for one.)

Although Patricia's book will especially appeal to collectors, I believe it will be of interest and benefit to others as well. Military history buffs should enjoy, in addition to the inscriptions and colorful military images featured on the pillow covers, Patricia's capsule comments about the military bases where the pillow covers were sold, as well as her brief accounts of some of the soldiers, sailors, and airmen who bought them and sent them home to loved ones. Also, cultural studies have in recent years expanded to include studies of popular literary texts examined in their connection to the ordinary folks who favored and read them; in Patricia's book students of popular poetry will find a great cache of humble "poems" (the word barely suffices) expressing devotion to Mother and conveniently assembled for study. And should any student of American culture feel an urge to ponder a possible deeper cultural meaning lurking in "Mother" pillow covers, Patricia's pages provide much raw material for that study. Indeed, perusing her pages, one finds that certain questions forcibly come to mind: Just how did those two titanic themes — Mom and war — ever get joined on pillow covers, and what does their linkage signify? Why, as appears to be the case, are "Mother" pillow covers uniquely an American institution? Why are American males the principal buyers and bestowers of "Mother" pillow covers?

These, in fact, are questions that I first posed in my article, which brings us back to the salient fact that no advance in the full cultural study of "Mother" pillow covers has been made during the past forty years. Will that situation change now? At least that possibility exists, thanks entirely to this valuable product of Patricia Cummings' great dedication and hard work. In the meantime, any reader of her book should find ample pleasure simply in gazing upon and marveling at the unusual tokens of Americana that fill her pages.

~~~~~~~

Lyell Henry is Emeritus Professor of Political Science at Mount Mercy College, where he taught from 1982 until retiring in 1999. Prior to 1982, he held administrative positions at Princeton University and the University of Iowa. He has a B.A. from Princeton University and an M.A. and Ph.D. from the University of Iowa, all three degrees in political science. He lives with his wife, Gretchen Holt, in Iowa City.

Henry is the author of two books, both published by the University of Iowa Press: *Zig-Zag-and-Swirl: Alfred W. Lawson's Quest for Greatness* (1991) and *Was This Heaven? A Self-Portrait of Iowa on Early Postcards* (1995). He has also written numerous articles in the fields of American popular culture, historic highways, and roadside commercial architecture. He is the historian on projects of restoration and interpretation at three Lincoln Highway sites in Iowa. Since 2001 he has also been a member of the state committee that reviews nominations from Iowa to the National Register of Historic Places.

~~~~~~~

"Man with Mother Pillow" is a portrait painting of Lyell D. Henry with a 'Mother' pillow. It was painted in 1971. *Courtesy of Joseph Patrick.*

Military Collectibles

*M*y discovery and purchase of a World War II rayon pillow cover in an antiques store a few years ago was just the start of a much larger collection — and this book! Fortuitously, while writing a series of articles about pillow covers for *The Quilter* magazine, I came across the work of Lyell D. Henry, who preceded me in writing about "Mother" pillows in 1971. He loaned me examples from his personal collection to photograph for an article. Later, upon learning that I had decided to write a book, he mailed me his entire collection of pillow covers, which represents three or four decades of gathering them!

Today, most folks draw a blank when asked if they know about "Mother" or "Sweetheart" pillows. Only dealers who clean out estates and try to sell items of this kind on the secondary market seem to be aware of them, except perhaps for military personnel. My sincere hope is that the public will not only gain an awareness of these textiles, but also that they appreciate them for the history they represent.

One person I came across questioned whether or not "those cheap, chintzy, and flimsy" textiles are a worthy topic. My reply would be the same today: "Each pillow cover is a little gem of history with information just waiting to be rediscovered. I have learned a tremendous amount of history because of them!"

Since the early twentieth century, members of the military could purchase a sentimental souvenir pillow cover at the PX or BX as a personal keepsake or to mail home. Most of the items shown in this book are from World War II. For the sake of consistency, they will be called "pillow covers," even though some folks may prefer to call them "pillow shams," "pillow slips," "pillow cases," "pillow cushion covers," or even "pillow throws." Of course, when a pillow cover is filled with stuffing or a pillow form, the proper term would be a "pillow."

Characteristics of "Mother" & Other Pillow Covers

Over the years, the materials used to construct pillow covers have varied, depending on the availability of raw materials. During World War I, felted wool or silk were the chosen fabrics. When rayon, the first man-made fabric, became widely available in America in 1925, it was "all the rage." During World War II, most pillow covers were rayon or a similar fabric called acetate. At times, we will see that rayon was used for the front and acetate for the back, or vice versa. Do not mistakenly call rayon a synthetic fiber. Synthetics are petroleum-based fibers such as nylon or polyester. Rayon is based on a combination of cotton linters and wood pulp, both "natural" fibers.

In this book, we will see a few other types of military collectibles made of rayon. These include scarves for women, as well as table covers, marked with the name of a military base; and non-absorbent souvenir handkerchiefs.

During World War I, fold-over pouches for "Sweetheart" and "Mother" were made of silk. However, during World War II, rayon replaced silk. The intended use of the pouches was to hold letters, hankies, or possibly lingerie (nylons were a scarce and prized commodity during wartime). The inside surface of the front flaps often features a sentimental poem and occasionally, the gift giver's signature.

Hand-painted portraits of famous people are sometimes seen on embroidered pillow covers from World War I. Some are heavily embroidered with flowers, flags, or the words "*Souvenir de France*." Outrageous prices are often asked in online auctions for these types of pillow covers. One eBay auction had a buy-it-now price of $400 dollars. Previously, a similar pillow cover was offered at twice that amount. Neither pillow sold.

Many pillow covers carry specific name designations that denote the relationship between the giver and the receiver. Poem titles feature the words "Sweetheart," "Mother," "Father," "Mother and Dad," "Wife," "Daughter," "Aunt," "Grandmother," or "Friend." At times the words "Remembrance," "Friendship," or "Forget Me Not" are present.

"Mom": The Inspiration for These Pillow Covers?

According to Lyell Henry's satirical essay that appears in Chapter One, the first pillow ever made by a soldier was for his "Mother." Due to his mention of the book *Generation of Vipers* by Philip Wylie, I wanted to know more, so I read Wylie's 1942 book. He discusses the concept of "momism," revealing that "megaloid momworship [sic] has got completely out of hand." Fellow quilters who have ever battled to grab up fabric at a hot, summer tent sale will be able to relate to Wylie's paragraph that appears on page 198:

"Much of the psychological material which got me studying the matter of moms came into my possession as I watched the flower-hatted goddesses battle over fabric. I have seen the rich and the poor, the well-dressed and the shabby, the educated and the unlettered, tear into the stacked remnants day after day, shoving and harassing, trampling each other's feet, knocking hats, coiffures and glasses awry, cackling, screaming, bellowing, and giving the elbow, without any differential of behavior no matter how you sliced them."

This opinion of moms seems to be in direct conflict with the images of "Mother" on these pillow covers. In a number of World War I pillow cover examples, Mother is presented as very home-y and sweet, sharing a "fond embrace" and standing proud while a service flag, proof that she

has a soldier son, waves behind her. The image calls to mind the type of Mom who would bake apple pies and leave them on a window sill to cool and who would knit socks and mittens for a cold winter's day.

If we fast-forward to World War II, we see a totally different view of Mom. She has joined the work force, traipsing off to work daily and leaving her children to become latchkey kids. If a painting by Norman Rockwell, which appeared on the cover of the *Saturday Evening Post*, September 4, 1943, is any indication, "Mom" became the gardener, the fisherman, the milk delivery "man," the auto mechanic, the nurse, the photographer, the plumber, the policeman (i.e., "policewoman"), and more.

My friend, Joan Kiplinger (1933-2009), was just eight years old in 1941 when World War II started and just twelve when the war ended in 1945. She sent me an e-mail on May 31, 2007, in which she reminisces about how her mother went off to work every day and what the general conditions were like during the war. In part, she says:

"Mom worked in a small appliance firm which converted to war production. It was on the next street. She looked so smart in her slack suit and snood [a type of head covering] and wedgies, walking to work with the other women on the street. Later, she worked at a little place called Thompson Products which by the end of the war had moved to California and became the giant Thompson Ramos Woodridge–TRW."

In a World War I postcard, *"carte postale,"* a young man sits at a table while he writes a letter to his mother, her face in his mind (and shown on the postcard itself in an elevated position in the top left corner).

"Seems like yesterday we were trudging the "hills" of Cleveland with our wagons to collect scrap metal and foil from cigarette packs. Or knitting squares at school to give to Red Cross groups, which then made them up into afghans, scarves, and hats; or saving our dimes in a folder that, when filled, bought a war bond. And keeping a solid watch on two elderly German women on our street whom we were convinced were spies, and many other memories. There was always someone connected to the Black Market to get you sugar, butter, or meat. Ration books did not go far for food or shoes or gas."

Some mothers, while hard at work on the home front, lost more than one son as a casualty of war. Against the backdrop of personal sacrifice and additional duties, mothers would have welcomed any word from a loved one in the service, but a "Mother" pillow cover, no doubt, would have been treasured.

Producing the Pillows

Natural Fibers Used in Pillow-Making

Most World War I military pillow covers are silk, wool, or, less often, leather. The latter two often feature brief words such as "U.S. Army" or "Quartermaster." Tan color, wool pillow covers are more common than more showy ones in red, white, and blue that are more likely to elicit eBay bidding wars. They also customarily reap more than $50 dollars. The lucky person will be able to purchase a wool pillow from the World War I era that has no moth holes, a rare find, indeed!

One memorable World War II pillow features the name "U.S. Army Tank Corps" and was posted several years ago in an online auction. On top of a tank, a wildcat wears a helmet. The seller states that the wildcat is the mascot for the U.S. Army's 81st Infantry Division. In Chapter Eleven, a military badge is shown from the same 81st Infantry Division. The pillow is further decorated with the World War I slogan "Treat 'em Rough."

Weighted silk seems to have been used in the manufacture of the now fragile pillow covers from World War I. New shipments of silk to the United States was interrupted by a civil war in China in 1910, which may be one possible explanation why inferior silk may have been used. Existing supplies, leftover from the late Victorian Era, may have been utilized. Of course, the long-term effect of weighting silk was not known until much more time had passed.

Today, shredding silk can be seen on Crazy Quilts from the 1880s and 1890s, a result of weighting silk by soaking it in arsenic, tin, or other metallic salts. Silk will readily absorb those substances causing it to weigh more when dry. This practice proved to be a major benefit to sellers, since silk was sold by the pound.

The Names of Manufacturers

Manufacturers were not required to add an identification tag to pillow covers to specify their name or the fiber contents. Rarely do we see pillow covers with a tag. Of the hundreds of pillow covers that I have examined, only six recorded names appear on tags that were visible near interior seams or on the face of the pillow cover itself. Companies that provided identification are: 1) "B.B. Company," 2) "Velvograph," 3) "GEMSCO; New York," 4) "SEEMOR PRODUCTS, St. Louis, Missouri," 5) "ANCO," and 6) "NS@CO." In addition, the company name, "SP & N Company, New York," is printed on a 1917 silk pillow pouch shown in Chapter Eight.

One textile previously shown on eBay is a U.S. Air Force pillow cover from World War II, made by "Artistic Spraying and Painting Co., 87 Greene St., New York, New York," that also shows a handwritten date of August 18, 1942. Another U.S. Army pillow cover from World War I, seen online, has a tag on the back that identifies its maker as "The Line of Art, The Chessler Company in Baltimore, Maryland." With the countless pillow covers manufactured during World War II alone, there must have been many other businesses involved.

Ironically, a few tags say "Made in Japan." Those pillow covers are notable for the use of black "spun rayon" fabric that serves as a background for poems, or in one case, for a nighttime image of the *U.S.S. Arizona* (monument) at Pearl Harbor. The pillow is a grim reminder of the more than 1,000 souls who lost their lives when that battleship was bombed and sunk on December 7, 1941, "a day that will live in infamy," according to President Franklin Delano Roosevelt. Pillow covers of this type may have been manufactured after the war in "Occupied Japan." The United States and Allied Forces were a continuing presence in Japan from the time the World War II peace treaty was signed on September 2, 1945 until April 28, 1952.

The ubiquitous, rainbow hued rayon pillow covers of World War II comprise the bulk of the military collectibles that Lyell Henry and I have collected. Since he began to gather examples for his collection, prices have risen dramatically. Value depends on condition, pleasing graphics and colors, and rarity.

The Civilian Conservation Corps

Between the wars, during the 1930s to the early 1940s, "Mother," "Mother and Dad," and other pillow covers were sold to members of the Civilian Conservation Corps for only $1 dollar each. That may not seem like a large amount today, but at the time, $1 dollar represented one-fifth of the recruit's monthly pay (i.e. the portion he was allowed to keep). The remainder of the pay, $25 dollars, went straight home to the family. As a point of comparison, an original sales tag, stapled to the upper corner of a World War II pillow cover, indicates a price of $7.50. If a mailing envelope was needed, the price rose by thirty cents.

Comparative Prices & Prices Today

"Measuring Worth," a website run by Samuel H. Williamson, President, and Lawrence H. Officer, Director of Research, provides points of comparison for monetary values. Using the Consumer Price Index calculator available at www.measuringworth. com, I determined that $7.50 in 1944 — the price of an Army "Sweetheart" pillow cover — would have an equivalent value of $91.40 in 2009 (the latest year result available). Using the same comparison tool, $1 dollar spent in 1935 for a pillow cover bought at a Civilian Conservation Camp, is equal to $15.60 today. One can have a lot of fun at the site, keying in various years and price values.

Quality pillow covers often slip by unnoticed by potential Internet buyers and may sell for a low starting price such as ninety-nine cents on eBay. Naturally, sellers hope that buyers will "bid it up." The lowest amount I paid for any pillow cover in this book is ninety-nine cents. With the shipping price set at $4.01, the total payment was only $5 dollars — a real bargain!

One reason for writing this price guide is to assist the growing number of collectors who wish to preserve these textile pieces of history, as well as know more about them. As more and more widows of former World War II soldiers leave their houses for nursing homes, additional collectible pillow covers that have been hidden away in dresser drawers for years will become available. Family members may be surprised that these items even exist!

Distinguishing Between WWI & WWII Pillow Covers

There are a few distinguishing factors between World War I and World War II pillow covers. Ones from "The Great War" (World War I) rarely show the relationship between the sender and the recipient. The word "Mother" may be present, but most World War I textiles lack the poetry that is frequently seen on World War II counterparts. Instead, graphic images are often present: flags, images of "Lady Liberty" or "Lady Columbia," an eagle: the U.S. Army insignia, or scenes of doughboys. On World War I pillow covers, a few lines about "Victory" may be present or the initials, "U.S.A.," or slogans such as "Over the Top."

Final Tributes

During World War II, 400,000 American military members perished out of the estimated 60 million casualties of the war. One can imagine a pillow cover mailed from a military base just before a soldier left for danger on distant shores. It could have been the last point of contact with a loved one, and a keepsake.

A headline, "Discovery of WWII sub brings closure to relative of Castle Rock sailor," introduces an article by Tony Lystra, published in *The Daily News Online* on March 24, 2010. The reporter reveals that the final resting place of Seaman Waite Hoyt Daggy was recently discovered. The unfortunate soul was on-board a submarine when it sank near the Philippines in August 1944. Lystra notes, "There may be, stored away somewhere, a satin pillow mailed to his mother from Hawaii."

Lystra further adds that, other than the [imagined] pillow, all that remains of Daggy is his name inscribed on a monument and a few photos. It is eye-opening to think of the potential importance of a textile of this kind. We can never fully appreciate the sentimental value these colorful, patriotic, and heartwarming pillows had for their recipients!

A Journey into History

In this book, we will look at close to 250 military textiles, mostly pillow covers. Research to discover the meaning of these textiles has been a terrific journey in learning about American history, world events, and important military and world leaders. I never grow weary of seeing the plethora of different pillow designs that exist. One will notice that some poems repeat. When that is the case and the poem already has been featured in its entirety, subsequent references will cite only the first two lines, followed by enclosed brackets to indicate that the poem is longer in its original form.

A Guide to Notations in the Captions

Disclaimer: Any attempt at pricing antiques or vintage textiles is subjective.

The price range provided with each caption reflects current expected market prices for items in similar condition. Estimates are based on the actual prices paid for recently purchased items, or final prices observed in online auctions and other sales pages. On the market, prices are variable due to general economic factors or even the season of the year. For example, the Internet is less active during the summer, when people spending more time outdoors or are away on vacation, but it is more active once school is back in session.

If participating in online auctions, be alert to shipping amounts. Sometimes, sellers set outrageously high shipping costs as a way to compensate them for any anticipated losses, should auctions not do well. If you are a seller, try to keep your costs reasonable. Otherwise, potential bidders may be discouraged from even placing an initial bid.

Overinflating the value of an object can be another problem. If someone purchases an item, based only on a description, disappointment may ensue when the purchase arrives. This is particularly true if the backing fabric of a pillow cover has mildew or mold. Note that a disagreeable odor usually indicates the presence of microorganisms.

An online bidder relies on photos and the seller's knowledge of a product. Often, antique dealers who deal with a wide variety of merchandise and are not textile specialists will describe a pillow cover's fiber content incorrectly, or give incorrect advice as to how to improve its condition. For example, many times rayon is called "silk" or sellers tell the buyer just "to iron" the item, which is usually poor advice, as I will explain in Chapter Nine.

When only a portion of the object is visible in a digital photo, request additional photos. Perhaps the seller is trying to hide the fact that a pillow cover is faded, ripped, stained, or has holes. Finally, be wary of those who insist that "all sales are final." Reputable sellers will stand by their products.

In this book, all pillows and pillow covers have been measured edge to edge, not including fringe, unless otherwise noted. In the case of World War I pillow covers, the fringe widths are provided, if only to point to the fact that they were extraordinarily long! This can be one clue as to a World War I provenance! Fringe measurements are not noted for pillow covers from any other time period, as they are more uniformly short, averaging a couple of inches. However, in the case of exceptionally short fringes on several World War II pillow covers, that information will be recorded.

Vintage Pillow Covers Show Fading & Wear

In their heyday, these pillow covers must have been a delight to receive! Those textiles that saw actual use as stuffed pillows have sustained some damage. Contact and friction can cause flocked lettering and decorations to wear off, and rayon fabric itself is not sturdy, sometimes becoming dislodged from the protective edge fringe. At the very least, most pillow covers exhibit fold lines from being kept in dresser drawers. Luckily, many of these textiles were never used and remain in absolutely pristine condition.

WWI: A Change in World Order

World War I marked the termination of world order, as it had been since the Napoleonic Wars, which lasted from 1799 to 1815. An invasion of Serbia began the war that was fought in Europe from the summer of 1914 until November 11, 1918 (Armistice Day). The fighting spread to Africa and the Pacific Islands. The United States did not get involved in the war until April 6, 1917. With an Allied victory at the end of the war, four strong empires had been overtaken: the German Empire, the Russian Empire, the Ottoman Empire, and the Austro-Hungarian Empire.

Called "The Great War," the First World War gained the name, "The War to End All Wars." The second most fatal war in history, with 15 million people dead, World War I did not prove to be the end of war. As history proved, the end of conflict was too great a charge for humankind.

Notice the patriotic themes and love of country that emanate from the charming pillow covers that date from World War I. The artistry of World War I silk pillow covers is so distinctive as to make them recognizably connected to that early twentieth century time period. "Mother" is the central theme of many of these special textiles, as you shall see. These pillow covers seem to represent "yesteryear," a coming of age of the United States when we were still defining our national identity and the essence of what it means to be Americans.

The rayon and acetate pillow covers from the 1930s and 1940s are no less important than if they were made of the finest silk. We can appreciate these textile objects as objects of material culture and for their impact at the time. They provided a non-threatening way for the men who were called to war to express their love and longing for those left at home. Today, these textiles provide a point of departure into the re-discovery of history itself and for that reason alone, they are valuable parts of American cultural artifacts.

Chapter One

A Look Back

The Significance of Mother Pillows in American History and Culture

By Lyell D. Henry

Reprinted from The Journal of Popular Culture, 1971

In considering the strangely neglected topic of "Mother" pillows, the student of American culture need not pause long to assure himself that it is a subject *multum in parvo*. Perhaps it is the very ubiquity of "Mother" pillows that has caused them to go unnoticed by scholars. Yet these tokens of sentiment (see Tables 1 and 2, pgs. 15-16), which have been taken so unreservedly into the hearts and homes of millions of Americans, deserve much closer study than they have so far gotten. The purpose of this article is not to provide that definitive study, but rather, as a prolegomenon, to sketch some features of "Mothers" pillows, which preliminary research has already brought to light and to indicate some lines which future research might fruitfully follow. It is hoped that other scholars will be sufficiently persuaded of the cultural importance of "Mother" pillows to contribute new inputs to their study and to help bring into sharper focus their full significance in American history and culture. At this point the research opportunities are great, and the field is wide open for the penetration of literally whole squads of scholars.

The earliest use of "Mother" pillows, which has been identified to-date, occurred during the War of 1812. At that time, one Abner McDonough of Wilmington, Delaware, was a private in the U.S. Army, stationed in Washington, D.C., almost on the eve of the siege of the capital by the British. In a letter sent to his mother dated August 12, 1813, he wrote as follows:

Some of us fellows took ahold [sic] of a good idea, Sunday week, which has led us to make special remembrances for our loved ones back home. We was wondering what to do with the sacks the feed for the mules comes in, and their being a lull in the fighting hereabouts and us having some time free for achange [sic], we got us some needles and coloured threads and sewed words of true sentiment, and designs too, on the sacks, then stuffing them with pine needles and sewing up the end. My pillow is for you, it says SWEETEST MOTHER, and has two harts [sic] on the ends. You will get it soon, as Johnny Adams of the 3rd reg. gets his discharge tomorrow and will deliver it to you in Wilm.[1]

Regrettably, the location of the pillow, if it even exists today, is not known. We do know, however, that within six months of writing this letter, Pvt. McDonough was killed on the field of battle. It is a sad twist of fate that he died from wounds received when he was kicked in the head by an army mule.

The most diligent research has not produced evidence of any further use of "Mother" pillows until during the Civil War,[2] when it was a fairly widespread practice among both the Northern and the Southern armies to send battlefront souvenirs, including an occupational "Mother" or "Sweetheart" pillow, home to loved ones. These pillows were usually made in the manner described above by Pvt. McDonough. Of course, throughout the entire nineteenth century, it was also the practice of young ladies to make samplers, a few of which have references to "Mother." However, "Mother" references were uncommon, and the dominant themes in samplers were usually "Home, Sweet Home" or statements of religious aspiration or sentiment. The samplers of this period are really a separate development and not too closely connected to the origin or evolution of "Mother" pillows.

"Mother" pillows, it is apparent, seem to rise in use during times of war, primarily due to their favor by military personnel on active duty.[3] Though the Spanish American War was of relatively short duration, "Mother" pillows again made their appearance. However, there is a fact of decisive importance about the "Mother" pillows of this period: a great many of them, perhaps most, were mass-produced in factories and then sold in military bases. Exactly how and why these important innovations occurred at this time is not known and would be an extremely interesting problem for intensive investigation. The scholarly yield of this one project could be unusually significant, for from this period on (i.e., from the time of the Spanish American War) virtually all "Mother" pillows were made and sold in large volume by commercial enterprises. On the pillows of this period, too, began to appear some of the themes, symbols, and expressions of mother love that were to become *de rigueur* for pillows made in all later periods.

But if the turn of the century was the critical period in the development of "Mother" pillows, it is clear that the Golden Age really began in 1917 with the United States' entry into World War I. Statistics kept by the Federation of American Retailers of Felt Products and Novelties (FARFPAN) reveal how huge a volume of "Mother" pillows was sold during the period 1917-1920. The Federations' statistics (see Table 1) also show how the market for "Mother" pillows declined in the interwar period (though a respectable average of about half a million continued to be sold every year from 1921 to 1940) and how sales soared again during World War II and the immediate post-war period. Predictably, sales fell off again in the 1950s (after the Korean War) and the first half of the 1960s. Surprisingly, however, the Vietnam War has not stimulated sales of "Mother" pillows.

This atypical relationship between the Vietnam War and the sale of "Mother" pillows deserves close study, for it may indicate that important changes are occurring in American character and lifestyles in the last third of the twentieth century. It may even indicate that the American public's emotional response to the Vietnam War is different from its response to past American wars. But one hesitates to go too far out on this particular limb until all the data is in. Clearly, if we are to gain insight into these crucial matters, scholars should begin at once to mount multifaceted inquiries into the points of interface between "Mother" pillows and the Vietnam War.

It would be impossible to track down and categorize the whole panoply of themes, images, and symbols that have appeared on "Mother" pillows.[4] Yet the need to deal with the thematic and symbolic content of "Mother" pillows remains; some effort in that direction must be made if we are to achieve closure in our analysis. Systematic sampling is ruled out, inasmuch as there is no known or fixed universe of "Mother" pillows from which a valid sample could be drawn. Therefore, the writer of this paper has had to utilize an alternative, which is, admittedly, methodologically flawed, but which will at least yield enough data to allow a preliminary sorting out of the rich thematic content of "Mother" pillows. That method is to measure the incidence of the more prominent themes that appear on the "Mother" pillows in the enormous collection in the halls of the Federation of American Mothers in Washington, D.C. Obviously, no excessive claims can be made for the results obtained. On the other hand, *nil desperandum*; they may at least fill several lacunae in our knowledge and lay the basis for future, more methodologically *avancé* investigations by other scholars. If so, these poor bricks of data will have made their worthy contribution to the construction of the temple of knowledge.

Table 2 summarizes the frequency and context of some of the most prominent characterizations of Mother found on "Mother" pillows in different time intervals. Since the linkage of "Mother" pillows to wars is clear, these intervals have been defined so as to

Amusing Footnote: Carl Bode, now deceased, was a "big name" in American Studies and a professor at the University of Maryland at the time Lyell D. Henry's article was published in 1971. To add a little fun to the topic himself, Bode wrote a short article titled, "Fluffing the "Mother" Pillow." This appeared in the next edition of *The Journal of Popular Culture* (Vol. 5, Issue 2, Fall 1971). Calling Henry's article "classic" and "only to be compared with H. L. Mencken's definitive if capsule history of the bathtub," Bode interjects that perhaps Henry means "Moth-er" instead of "Mother" pillows because mothballs came into wide use in the 1870s and were used to stuff the pillows. He also suggests, among other things, that the statistics in Table 1 "are off, though merely by a million or two." Henry welcomed this response and enjoyed the good-natured chiding of his colleague.

highlight major war and inter-war periods in modern U.S. history. Given the prolegomenetic intent of this paper, it is neither necessary nor possible to comment at length on the totality of important implications of the data presented in Table 2. However, some of the more salient conclusions will be identified.

First, the characterization of mother as "best girl," "true love," or "sweetheart" has appeared so frequently and constantly in all time periods as to make its inclusion on "Mother" pillows virtually a defining characteristic of the genus. Somewhat in contrast, mother characterized as vision of dreams or subject of prayers is a prominent but not nearly so universal a theme on "Mother" pillows in each time period.

It is in the case of the other three characterizations that shifts in incidence over time which are so dramatic as to raise a question about what they may signify. On the one hand, mother seen as the center of childhood memories has steadily become a more prominent theme on "Mother" pillows, going from an incidence of 41% in 1914-18 to a very high rate of 85% in the 1946-60 period. On the other hand, over the same span of time, the more abstract and militant characterizations of mother have fallen off sharply. The incidence rate of mother as a force inspiring victory over U.S. enemies goes from 74% to a, by contrast, paltry 9%. The rate of incidence of mother as the embodiment of the noblest ideals and values of American civilization falls off even more strikingly — from 84% to 7%.

Surely these remarkable patterns have a meaning that it behooves students of American culture to probe deeply! It is not a purpose of this paper to tease out that deeper meaning, but it can at least be asked in passing whether the decline in idealistic and militant characterizations of mother in the recent period is an index of a shift in the American *Weltanschauung* or at least a decline in patriotic fervor, which many critics allege has occurred among today's youth. Is it also possible that this trend measures, as well as any other indicator known, an imminent decline of American civilization (in some ultimate, Toynbean sense)? But, tempting as the opportunity is, no more will be said about the possible meanings of the changing content of "Mother" pillows. This section will have accomplished its goal if it does no more than convince most readers that there is a crying need for study of these trends by the most capable minds which American scholarship could provide.[5]

This paper has already suggested several important aspects of "Mother" pillows, which are sorely in need of more research and may have great spin-off value for the whole field of American studies. Some of these aspects have to do with specific episodes in the history of the development and use of "Mother" pillows, but some relate more basically to questions about American culture and character. Three major questions of the latter sort are: (1) Why are "Mother" pillows uniquely an American phenomenon?; (2) Why are they so peculiarly associated (in their origin and in their heaviest use) with wars?; and (3) Why are American males the principal buyers and bestowers of "Mother" pillows?[6] and, of course, *ut supra*, scholars should undertake at once to determine what changes may be occurring in the historic patterns of use of "Mother" pillows and to offer reasoned and documented explanations for those changes.

There are other aspects of "Mother" pillows that should be considered, too. For instance, nothing has been said in this paper about the aesthetic or literary qualities of "Mother" pillows. Yet there is room for at least one Ph.D. candidate in American literature to undertake a comprehensive study of the poetry found on "Mother" pillows.[7] An even more fertile field for scholars is "Mother" pillows considered as an art form. The same broad-minded contemporary spirit, which has secured a critical recognition for such popular art forms as fraternal lodge badges, gum cards, neon store signs, plaster lawn figurines, and comic books, should now be directed towards "Mother" pillows. The effort could be productive of many journal articles for enterprising *Gelehrten* in several disciplines.

This brief survey of research possibilities was not intended to be exhaustive. Other important questions about "Mother" pillows will doubtless occur to readers. It is the hope of the writer that these readers will follow up those questions with well-designed research efforts. He will feel gratified if others now join with him in mining the scholarly ore which lies untapped in the rich mother lode of "Mother" pillows.

Article Endnotes

Author's Note: All additional chapter endnotes are grouped at the end of the document.

1. From a letter in the Francis Scott Key Memorial Archives, Baltimore, Maryland.

2. This statement is strictly true, and yet one fact of related interest which turned up in research is worth reporting here. According to some unpublished notes (Niagra Weed Collections, Buffalo, New York) written by Thurlow Weed, the nineteenth century New York political boss, in 1842 Millard Fillmore, then Congressman from New York, commissioned a local cabinet-maker to make a settee to be presented by Fillmore to his mother. The settee was upholstered with a piece of cloth on which were embroidered the word "Mother" and representations of several species of flowers. At the death of his mother, Fillmore inherited the settee, and upon his ascension to the Presidency in 1850, he took it with him to the White

House where it was frequently seen and admired by visitors, especially those from foreign countries. Fillmore, of course, was also the first President to install and use a bath tub in the White House. (See H. L. Mencken, "A Neglected Anniversary," *New York Evening Mail*, December 28, 1917.)

3. Why military personnel favor "Mother" pillows is a question of capital importance and deserves much more attention than it has gotten from scholars. For a preliminary foray into a related area of importance, see the author's forthcoming article in *The Journal of Military Psychology* entitled "Pillow Fetishism in the U.S. Army during the Korean War."

4. The reference to "Mother" on "Mother" pillows is sometimes only that one word alone, but usually there is more, including phrases of sentiment of even whole poems signifying one's love and/or worship of mother, all of the above also usually being embellished with an outer tasseled fringe and with designs such as flowers, hearts, wreathes, eagles, and American flags. Other types of verbal content may sometimes be included. In particular, during World War I, slogans or epithets against the enemy were especially prevalent, e.g. "Hit the Hun!", "Death to the Heathen Hun!", or "Kaiser Bill, Go to Hell!" Similar sentiments appeared, although much less frequently, during World War II. Perhaps the most popular phrase of this type was "Zap a Jap for Mom."

5. Any future work by scholars on the cultural significance of "Mother" pillows will sooner or later have to come to terms with Philip Wylie's seminal study of "Momism" (see his *Generation of Vipers*, New York: Rinehart, 1942, pp. 184-204). Nowhere in his analysis of Momism does Wylie deal directly with "Mother" pillows, yet everywhere there are (hints of) ideas which might be employed in their study. There is a caveat to be observed in the use of Wylie's analysis, however, his work suffers from his use of a method which is not notably *wissenschaftlich* and in fact is value impregnated, impressionistic, even journalistic and satiric. Scientific scholars will first need to operationalize his definitions and subject his conclusions to rigorous testing by the use of the most advanced methodology before his ideas can be used with any confidence.

6. The writer has been told by an informant at the University of California that the so called "research department" of a West Coast chapter of the Women's Liberation movement is preparing a monograph on "abnormal masculine traits" which includes material on "the male fondness for "Mother' pillows." However this particular way of characterizing the topic will doubtless skew the research findings to an unacceptable degree. In any event, advance reports indicate that the monograph is so polemical (and foul mouthed, it may be added) as to be almost useless for scholarly purposes.

7. A representative poem (taken from a pillow in the writer's collection) is as follows: "MOTHER / She's a lot of fun to be with / She's peppy and she's sweet, / She's always understanding / She's a pal who's hard to beat. / And I have loved her very much / Since I was very small, / For my Mom is a darling / and she really tops them all." Poetry of this type has never received the attention it deserves, perhaps because critics have been too ready to judge it by formal aesthetic criteria rather than in terms of its functional relationship to its typical readers. The study of "Mother" pillows therefore offers an enterprising scholar an excellent chance to challenge the elitist standards which have arrested poetic criticism for so long.

TABLE 1

NUMBERS OF "MOTHER" PILLOWS SOLD DURING DIFFERENT TIME PERIODS*

TIME PERIOD	NUMBER SOLD (IN MILLIONS)
1917 - 20[†]	12.3
1921 - 25	2.9
1926 - 30	2.7
1931 - 35	2.7
1936 - 40	2.6
1941 - 45	11.7
1946 - 50	5.1
1951 - 55	3.6
1956 - 60	2.8
1961 - 65	2.7
1966 - 70	2.6

*Data Source: Federation of American Retailers of Felt Products and Novelties (FARFPAN).
[†]No statistics available for years prior to 1917.

Table 1, Number of "Mother" Pillows Sold During Different Time Periods.

TABLE 2

CHARACTERIZATIONS OF MOTHER FOUND ON "MOTHER" PILLOWS IN DIFFERENT TIME PERIODS*

CHARACTERIZATION OF MOTHER	PERCENT OF PILLOWS IN TIME PERIOD CONTAINING CHARACTERIZATION[†]			
	1914-18	1919-40	1941-45	1946-60
As "best girl," "true love," "sweetheart," etc.	96%	94%	97%	95%
As force inspiring victory over U. S. enemies	74%	11%	39%	9%
As center of childhood memories	41%	60%	89%	85%
As embodiment of noblest values, ideals of American civilization	84%	37%	49%	7%
As vision of dreams, subject of prayers	35%	31%	35%	37%

*Data source: Federation of American Mothers collection, Washington, D. C.
[†]Characterization may be presented in words and/or visual imagery.

Because pillows usually contain more than one characterization of mother, the percentages in each column do not total to 100%

Table 2, Characterizations of Mother Found on "Mother" Pillows in Different Time Periods.

Drawing of two pillows by Lyell D. Henry.

Chapter Two

World War I & Souvenir Pillow Covers

In the fictitious account you just read in Chapter One, you will recall that the author, Lyell Henry, states that the earliest "pillow" on record is one from 1813. In actuality, pillow covers to commemorate military events seem to have come into use just before World War I and were available to a much greater extent during World War II. Some exist from the Korean Conflict and we have reports that at least a few were available during the Vietnam War, ostensibly embroidered in Vietnam. However, World War II marked the most abundant manufacture of textiles of this type.

"The Punitive Expedition"

The silk pillow cover featured in this section is important because of its connection to General "Jack" Pershing. Eventually, he would hold the highest military rank ever bestowed upon anyone: "General of the Armies." In 1976, General George Washington was given the same title by an Act of Congress.

John Joseph "Blackjack" Pershing distinguished himself as a soldier during the so-called "Indian Wars," the Spanish-American War, the Mexican Expedition, and World War I. The reason for his nickname, "Blackjack" Pershing was that he had once served as commander of the African American 10th Cavalry.[1]

Prior to the Mexican "Punitive Expedition," Pershing met the infamous José Oroteo Arango Arámbula, better known as "Francisco Villa" or "Pancho Villa," at the U.S. Army base at Fort Bliss, Texas. Ultimately, Pershing would lead troops in pursuit of Villa and his band of rebels. Villa's men, under the command of General Ramón Banda Quesada, attacked the town of Columbus, New Mexico, burning it down and killing both soldiers and civilians.

In 1915, Pershing had hoped to move his wife and children to Fort Bliss. Instead, he received the tragic news that his wife, Frances Warren, whom he had married in 1905, and three of their four children had succumbed to smoke inhalation during a hotel fire.[2]

The only son to survive the tragedy, Colonel Francis Warren Pershing (1909-1980), served as an advisor to General George C. Marshall during World War II. "Jack" Pershing's two grandsons both served in the military as well: Richard W. Pershing (1942-1968), who was an officer of the 402nd Infantry, was killed in action in Vietnam on February 17, 1968, while the other grandson, Colonel John Warren Pershing III (1941-1999), developed Reserve Officer Training Corps (ROTC) programs for the Army and died a natural death.[3]

In 1932, John J. Pershing wrote a two volume, autobiographical account titled, *My Experiences in the World War*, a book that won the Pulitzer prize for History writing.

This rare silk pillow cover from the U.S. Army is a tribute to a famous general, John Joseph Pershing. The poem says: "We'll be after you, Jack Pershing / In just a little while! / Democracy is marching now, / in column, mile on mile / We'll be ready for your orders, Jack / We love that good old smile / So look for us, Jack Pershing / in just a little while." This pillow cover has a brown 4" fringe. 15.75" x 17". 1917-1918. $60-75.

When this item was received, it was clear that it had come into contact with black cat fur, traces of which clung to the front surface. The back was badly stained, perhaps the victim of spraying by the same animal. Luckily, there must have been a pillow form inside that absorbed the liquid, as no organic stains can be seen on the front, which appears to be in nearly perfect condition. There is but one additional small stain, the size of a pencil eraser, on the left bottom front. Without the cat hair, this item is in improved condition.

This silk pillow cover features a photo transfer of the face of General John Joseph Pershing, enhanced by silk embroidery. It is still in excellent condition. Roses are embroidered with various shades of violet, pink, and white silk threads. The hat and uniform are embroidered, as are the words "*Souvenir de France*" and "General Pershing." The French flag and the American flag are displayed together to show the unity of the two countries in their counteroffensive against the Germans. A heavy, metallic, corded trim is used for surface decoration just inside the edges of the pillow cover. A fancy lace edge is used to finish this item. 18.625" x 17". 1917-1918. $60-75.

Military Units Terminology

Let's review the various names of military units. Traditionally speaking, a *squad* is the smallest unit, with four to ten men led by a staff sergeant. A *platoon* is a collection of three or four squads led by a lieutenant. A *company* consists of three or four platoons, led by a captain. A *battalion* usually has three or more companies, led by a lieutenant colonel. Three battalions or more are led by a full colonel. A *division* is led by a major general, and a *brigade* is a combination of a few infantry divisions. Many thanks to Kristin Henderson, who wrote *While They're at War: The True Story of American Families on the Homefront*, for clarifying these terms in her book. She notes that these descriptions of units are in a state of flux, with no strict adherence in recent conflicts. We will certainly run across these military terms in the pillow cover descriptions!

During the Mexican Revolution, Francisco "Pancho" Villa was enraged that the United States recognized the national government of Mexico led by Venustiano Carranza. Villa crossed over the U.S.-Mexican border to lead raids. On March 9, 1916, his men attacked the U.S. 13th Cavalry in Columbus, New Mexico, leaving a total of twenty-six military men and civilians killed or wounded. Pershing, promoted to Brigadier General by President Theodore Roosevelt, took over the command of the U.S. Army's 8th Cavalry Regiment at Fort Bliss, Texas. He led this regiment of the American Expeditionary Forces (A.E.F.) into Mexico in March 1916 in an attempt to catch Pancho Villa. The effort failed.[4]

A "service flag" is featured at the center top of this patriotic pillow cover from World War I. These small textiles were given to families to hang in windows. If one member of the family was serving in the military, one star would be present. Additional stars would be added, depending on the number of loved ones serving. In a travesty of justice, one mother lost five of her sons, at the same time, during World War II.

The famous "Sullivan" boys enlisted in the U.S. Navy with the stipulation that they be allowed to serve together. They died on November 13, 1942, when their battleship, the *U.S.S. Juneau*, was hit by a Japanese torpedo. Their ages ranged from twenty to twenty-seven. As a result of their deaths, new regulations were adopted to prevent a similar situation from occurring ever again.

The previous owner of this pillow cover was Reverend Bart C. Trexler (who died in 2004). He belonged to the West Point Chapter of the Company of Military Historians and enjoyed collecting artifacts from the Civil War and World War II.

An interesting tribute to him, discovered on the Internet, retells the story of how he obtained the pillow cover. While on a vacation trip to Gettysburg, Pennsylvania, Bart's wife reminded him that he had reached his pre-set spending limit set for antiques. After making one last stop along the way, he spotted a Navy Confederate flag that he could not leave behind. He purchased it for $35 dollars, but later sold it to a Confederate museum for $8,300.[5]

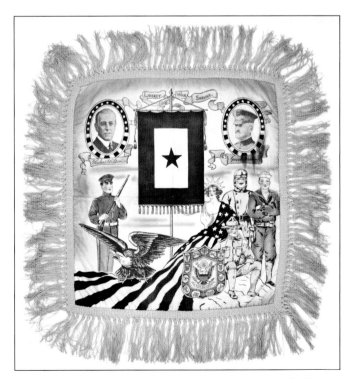

This silk pillow cover features graphic photos images of Major General John ("Jack") Joseph Pershing and Woodrow Wilson, who served as U.S. president from 1913 to 1921. A flag is draped over the shoulder of Lady Liberty. This has a 4" greenish tan fringe. 15.75" x 17.125". 1917. $40-50.

This U.S. Army silk pillow cover is rare because of its round shape. Named images from the "Mexican Expedition" (also known as the "The Punitive Expedition" of 1916-1917) include: 1) "A Camp Scene," 2) "On the Firing Line," and 3) "Firing at the Enemy." A cartouche at the bottom features the words "Greetings from the Mexican Borders [sic]." American flags are placed at top center, with an eagle, along with the letters "U.S.A." This pillow cover has slightly frayed silk at bottom center and some damage to the lovely 3" wide lace around its outer perimeter; its diameter is 20.75". 1916-1917. $75-100. *Courtesy Lyell D. Henry.*

The words "Camp Cody," which appear in the upper right corner, makes this pillow cover easy to date. This Camp did not exist before 1917. The writing looks like hand-painted cursive letters. The U.S. Army's 34th Infantry Division, nicknamed the "Sandstone Division," was stationed at this base in Deming, New Mexico, from 1916-1918. This unit was named for the famous buffalo hunter, "Buffalo Bill Cody." National Guardsmen were trained at this site and later deployed to France during World War I.[6]

The image of Lady Columbia graces another pillow cover from Camp Cody. She holds a wreath. The background color is light tan. An eagle in flight grasps olive branches in one talon and arrows in the other, a design that often repeats on objects of American material culture, especially textiles. The silk on one edge of the pillow is beginning to fray.

"Hail, Columbia!" is another silk U.S. Army pillow cover. "Camp Cody, Deming, New Mexico" appears in the upper right corner. One edge of the top is separated from the fringe. This has a 3.5" lavender fringe. 16.375" x 16.75". 1917-1918. $25-35. *Courtesy of Lyell D. Henry.*

Pastel colors adorn this silk "Sister" pillow cover from Camp Cody, New Mexico, a U.S. Army training camp established in 1917. This has a 4" light green, macramé type of fringe. The silk fabric is considerably frayed on two sides. 16" x 17.25". 1917-1918. $25-35. *Courtesy of Lyell D. Henry.*

This silk pillow cover prominently displays the words "World War On Autocracy" and features the insignia of five branches of the Army, in the points of a star that presents the words "Liberty" and "War Service." The flags of four countries are displayed: the United States, France, the United Kingdom, and Italy. The background of the pillow is a mottled mix of pastel colors, always a sure clue to twentieth century provenance, as pastel color dyes were not available until then. A small eagle holds a banner with the words "*e pluribus unum*," a Latin term that means "out of many, one." This saying appears on the Great Seal of the United States and reappears on many American textiles, especially military collectibles.

From World War I, this colorful pillow cover features the words "World War On Autocracy" and shows the flags of the United States, France, the United Kingdom, and Italy. The cloth may be a silk and cotton blend. There is one brown stain on the left side of the fringe that looks like ink. 16" x 16.75". This has a white 4" fringe. 1917-1918. $25-30.

The Liberty Bell, with an eagle resting on top, features a U.S. Army Corps insignia and the name, "Camp Forrest, Georgia." A soldier and a sailor stand ready on either side of the bell to protect and serve. A ribbon banner says, "For Liberty and Democracy."

During the Civil War, the original name of this site was "Camp Peay." The camp, located near Tullahoma, Tennessee, was renamed for Civil War General Nathan Bedford Forrest (1821-1877), a wealthy business owner and slave trader who was accused of war crimes against a Black Union Army division during the Civil War.[7] He served in the Confederate military from 1861-1865 and was a leader of the Ku Klux Klan. During World War II, Camp Forrest held Italian and German prisoners of war. In 1951, President Truman renamed the military installation as the "Arnold Engineering Development Center," in honor of Air Force General Henry H. "Hap" Arnold (1886-1950).

A U.S. Army silk pillow cover shows a soldier and a sailor standing on either side of a Liberty Bell. Light "foxing" on surface. Was this item previously kept in damp conditions? It has some shredded silk fibers, and a red stain at upper right. This has a 2.25" tan fringe. 19" x 16.25". 1917-1918. $15-25.

Origins of the Nickname "Doughboy"

Curious about the term "doughboy," the name for soldiers during World War I, distinguishable by the type of hat they wear, I looked up the term in *The New Oxford American Dictionary*. The first definition of "doughboy" is a boiled or deep-fried dumpling. However, the informal definition is that of a U.S. infantryman during World War I.

One theory is that "doughboy" originated during the American Civil War and came about because of the large globular brass buttons on infantry uniforms that resemble biscuits.[8] Furthermore, it has been stated that the term could have been derived from the use of pipe clay "dough," which was used to clean the soldiers' white belts.

The *Stars and Stripes* newsletter dated April 25, 1919, answers a question from a reader as to the origin of the name "doughboy." The response is this:

The word "doughboy" originated in the Philippines. After a long march over extremely dusty roads the Infantrymen came into camp covered with dust. The long hikes brought out the perspiration, and the perspiration mixed with the dust formed a substance resembling dough; therefore their lucky brothers, the mounted soldiers, called them "doughboys."[9]

Michael E. Hanlon, a member of the World War I Society, explores the background of the word and other theories behind the word in an online article titled, "The Origins of Doughboy, An Interim Report." He concludes that there is a lack of clear primary evidence to indicate when the term first became associated with the military. He indicates that the word "doughboy" may have been used in a pejorative way, at least at first, but during World War I it was adopted as "the universally popular nickname of all the American troops sent to Europe [...]."[10]

A doughboy is shown inside a star on this U.S. Army pillow cover from World War I. It features large letters, in black and lavender, that say "U.S.A." and are placed diagonally. Openings for the pillow insertion can be found on any one side of these covers. This one has an opening at the top. The beautiful backing fabric is silk and has motifs of bamboo trees and leaves on a "water" background. At the bottom, it says, "On to Victory," a slogan of World War I. Various insignia of branches of the U.S. Army are also represented. 16.25" x 17", with a 2.75" yellow-green fringe. 1916-1917. $50-75.

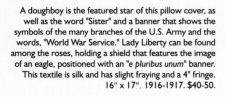

A doughboy is the featured star of this pillow cover, as well as the word "Sister" and a banner that shows the symbols of the many branches of the U.S. Army and the words, "World War Service." Lady Liberty can be found among the roses, holding a shield that features the image of an eagle, positioned with an "e *pluribus unum*" banner. This textile is silk and has slight fraying and a 4" fringe. 16" x 17". 1916-1917. $40-50.

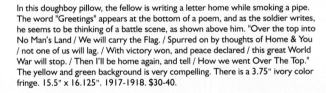

In this doughboy pillow, the fellow is writing a letter home while smoking a pipe. The word "Greetings" appears at the bottom of a poem, and as the soldier writes, he seems to be thinking of a battle scene, as shown above him. "Over the top into No Man's Land / We will carry the Flag. / Spurred on by thoughts of Home & You / not one of us will lag. / With victory won, and peace declared / this great World War will stop. / Then I'll be home again, and tell / How we went Over The Top." The yellow and green background is very compelling. There is a 3.75" ivory color fringe. 15.5" x 16.125". 1917-1918. $30-40.

The "America First" pillow cover features the words "Over the Top" at the bottom, a slogan of World War I. The image of doughboys was created by printing an actual photo on silk. Crossed rifles appear at the top right, and an eagle sitting on an American flag, is the motif on the left. This has a 3.75" rose color fringe. 15.75" x 17". 1917-1918. $25-40.

This pillow cover from World War I shows a charming scene in the center, but depictions of war outside the "star." Shown are 1) infantrymen charging into battle, holding a bayonet and an American flag, 2) three soldiers, one of whom is holding a bayonet with a bloody tip, 3) an armored Army tank and barbed wire, and 4) an American Bald Eagle ripping the heart out of another bird that represents Kaiser Wilhelm II (1859-1941), the last Kaiser of Germany. A crown and broken sword lie nearby. Interesting to note is the juxtaposition of war and love as represented by the images of this pillow cover.

The main motif of this U.S. Army pillow cover shows a mother and soldier ("doughboy") son saying goodbye. These words are written at the bottom: "A fond embrace, a Mother's kiss. / A loving son, what earthly bliss. / What e're their fate, two hearts entwined. / In loving memory thus enshrined." This has a 3" light blue and white fringe. 16.625" x 15.625". 1917-1918. $65-75. *Courtesy of Lyell D. Henry.*

This silk U.S. Army pillow cover depicts troops on the ground, plane in the air, a trailing ribbon that hosts various insignia, and a "service flag" with one star, which would have been displayed in a window to show that a family had one of their sons in the military. An eagle is present as are the words "World War Service." Although in poor condition, due to its shredding silk, this pillow cover continues to tell the story of World War I. There is a 4" light orange fringe. 16" x 16.75". 1917-1918. $15-20. *Courtesy of Lyell D. Henry.*

This WWI Army pillow cover with the words "When Duty Calls" has to be my favorite of the entire pillow covers collected so far. It repeats the theme seen on the World War I pillow cover that says "A fond embrace" featured in the previous photo, as it depicts a touching scene of a World War I soldier, wearing a doughboy hat, saying "farewell" to his gray-haired mother while troops march past. A service flag hangs on the porch and a faithful dog participates in saying goodbye. This has a 3.125" light green fringe, and is in perfect condition. 15.875" x 16.75". 1917-1918. $60-70.

Georges Benjamin Clemenceau (1841-1929) served twice as the Prime Minster of France, from 1906-1909 and again, from 1917-1920. He belonged to the Radical Party and was a medical doctor who, for a short time, practiced in New York City. As a journalist, he founded a weekly newsletter titled, *Le Travail*, and started his own newspaper, *La Justice*, in 1880 in Paris. He also founded several magazines.[11] As the leader of France during the last year of World War I, he helped to negotiate the Treaty of Versailles. He earned two nicknames during his lifetime, "Le Tigre" (the Tiger) and "le Père la Victoire" (Father Victory).[12]

Appointed as Prime Minister in November 1917, Clemenceau instilled a sense of improved morale among the soldiers by visiting them often in the trenches. He favored an all-out war that would result in victory with justice and included a plan to punish all those who had instigated crimes against France. In 1918, Allied Forces, backed by Americans, made it impossible for Germany to win the war.

The Germans ceased hostilities when they signed an armistice agreement on November 11, 1918. Clemenceau is credited as being a "strong, energetic, positive leader who was the key to the allied victory in 1918."[13] It is unusual to find a hand-painted tribute pillow made to honor an individual, but such is the case with Clemenceau. A biography was written about him titled *The Tiger: The Life of Georges Clemenceau 1841-1929* by E. Holt (London: Hamilton, 1976).

In the two-volume book, *My Experiences in the World War, Volume II,* by John J. Pershing, the author ends the book with this statement:

Upon my arrival in Paris that afternoon, I hastened over to call on M. Clemenceau. To my mind, he was the greatest of French civil officials. Thought some seventy-six years of age, he had the vigor, the fire, and the determination of a man of fifty. He will live long in history. I had not seen him since the cessation of hostilities and when we met he was much affected, and indeed demonstrative.

This hand-painted tribute portrait on silk celebrates the life of French statesman Georges Benjamin Clemenceau (1841-1929). Written inscriptions include: "*Souvenir de France*" and "*Honneur a Clemenceau.*" Like other imported French silk pillows, this has elaborate, wide, lace edges, and other signs that its maker was highly skilled in couture work. The center measures 9" x 9.625" and the composite border edges, including lace and ruffles, measure a total of 7.25". 23.5" x 23.5". 1918. $55-65.

We fell into each other's arms, choked up and had to wipe our eyes. We had no differences to discuss that day.[14]

"*Souvenir de France*" silk pillow covers are larger than most other collectible textiles of the type we have been considering. They are often hand embroidered with flowers and flags in silk thread. The wide lace edges offer intricate work. These were often mailed home by GIs serving in France or brought home at the end of the war. Be wary of those that are framed, as framing may have been done without the use of proper archival materials. Silk can be damaged by contact with non-archival paper or cardboard, which is not acid-free.

This is another "*Souvenir de France*". World War I silk pillow cover. It is hand-embroidered with floral designs worked in silk threads, on a silk background. Note: A pillow like this one, in very poor condition, was offered online for $150, but had no buyers. There was another "*Souvenir de France*" pillow offered for $700 as a "buy-it-now" auction, a totally-inflated price. That one did not sell, even though it was posted more than once. This pillow cover has a 3.625" lace edge. 25.25" x 23.50". 1918. $30-40.

The Bulldog in the center of this one-layer textile in polished cotton of a drab color represents the early British Empire. The Bulldog, a mascot of the United Kingdom, is surrounded by the flags of Ireland, Canada, New Zealand, Scotland, South Africa, Wales, and India while flocked banners announce the names of the countries. The perimeter again is decorated with flocked design motifs that resemble Grecian keys. The edges are fraying a bit just from being handled over the years. This is a rare war commemorative textile.

This polished cotton textile has only one layer and depicts the flags of the countries held by the early British Empire at the time. An English Bulldog stands atop a British flag. Curiously, the edges of this textile are printed somewhat askew. 17.875" x 17.375". Circa 1914. $50-60. *Courtesy of Lyell D. Henry.*

Camp McCoy, Wisconsin, was established in 1909. Formerly called Camp Robert Bruce McCoy, its name was abbreviated in 1926. The man whom it honors served as a General in the National Guard and lived from 1867 to 1926. By 1940, the Camp's land area comprised more than 61,000 acres. Two years later, the site had a capacity to house 35,000 men. The WACs (Women's Army Corps) joined the military site in May 1943. At the end of World War II, the Camp served as a "Reception and Separation Center."[15] Given the name Fort McCoy once again, the site is still in use today as a "Total Force Training Center."[16]

The scenes on this scarf depict both World War I and World War II, according to James Cummings, who dates most of the images as "Between the Wars." At the bottom, the single-winged airplanes indicate a post-World War I time period. The design of the tank is post-World War I, but not yet World War II. An old style Cavalry hat and a Springfield gun are thrown into the mix, apparently for effect. A water-cooled machine gun is shown, a type of gun that began to be phased out during the early part of World War II.

One commemorative textile is a beautiful pillow cover in silk that is printed on both sides. Four U.S. Navy battleships — the *U.S.S. New York, U.S.S. Wyoming, U.S.S. Pennsylvania*, and the *U.S.S. Texas* — are seen on the front of the textile. On that same side are the words "War of 1917" and "In Memory to my Service." Roses and flag motifs complement the overall nautical design layout. This fragile fabric would not have stood up to heavy use as a pillow, and luckily, it seems to have never been used for that purpose.

War scenes from both World War I and World War II can be seen on this rayon scarf that features the name "U.S. Army, Camp McCoy, Wisconsin." The edges have been serged on an overlock sewing machine, a type of sewing machine first invented circa 1881 by J. Makens Merrow of Connecticut and his son, Joseph Merrow. Though some of the armaments depict an earlier time, we believe that this was manufactured circa 1943. 23.125" x 23". $20-30.

This double-sided U.S. Navy printed pillow cover features a view of four battleships on one side. The reverse side shows a sailor near an anchor, and a woman beside an anchor. Between the two individuals is a flag and these words: "Remember Me. Sweet be to thee life's passing hours / And all thy path be decked with flowers." 23" x 23". 1917. $48-58.

This oversize silk pillow cover appears to be handmade at home. The four quadrant triangles of printed fabric feature the flags of nations along on its edges. A half-inch piece of ribbon is woven through a strip of finely woven trim that divides the triangles visually. The battleship *U.S.S. Vermont* and a partial view of the *U.S.S. Delaware* are seen. There is one small stain on the front and one small hole approximately one quarter inch in diameter.

This is a silk pillow cover with a red backing also made of silk that is brought from the back to the front of the textile, turned under, and stitched down. Made to honor battleships in the U.S. Navy, the printed words include "*U.S.S. Vermont* Battleship" and "The *Vermont* won the gunnery trophy at the Southern Drill Grounds 1909," as well as the poem: "Of all the ships of our great fleet, The *Vermont* could not be beat: / We certainly did it with our men and gun, / A steady aim, "Fire!" / And the Trophy is won." 22" x 22". Circa 1909. $20-30.

"Lady Columbia" or "Lady Liberty" is standing in front of a 48-star flag with the Sword of Justice in her right hand and two ribbons trailing from a partial laurel wreath. The words "Honor" and "Victory" are written on the ribbons. Biplanes can be seen flying while, on the ground, men are marching with bayonets, cannons are firing, and a battleship is in sight near the coast.

"For the Freedom of the World!" is the statement at the bottom of this patriotic silk pillow cover. This item is in extraordinarily good condition and features a 4" light olive (yellow-green) fringe. 16" x 17". 1917-1918. $25-40.

Today, the Naval Station in Brooklyn, New York, mentioned on this pillow cover is but a memory. Members of The Armed Guard Center were active during World War II, forming a presence on merchant vessels to protect them. They continued to serve as crew members until 1946.

This U.S. Navy silk pillow cover was described and sold as a "Disney Donald Duck Naval Pillow from World War II." The duck does not resemble "Donald Duck" and its beak looks more like that of a pelican. By the way, Donald Duck's official birth date is June 9, 1934. The silk used to make the pillow suggests that it is a World War I item. Scant information is available online about the U.S. Naval Station and The Armed Guard Center, Brooklyn, New York. This pillow cover has a couple of minor areas where the silk is shredding in vertical strands. 16.25" x 17.25". 1917-1918. $45-60.

When the United States entered World War I, the German ship *S.S. Vaterland* was docked in Hoboken, New Jersey, and was confiscated by the United States. Renamed the *U.S.S. Leviathan*, it became a transport ship that brought troops to Brest, France, and by war's end had delivered almost 120,000 troops there.

The *U.S.S. Leviathan* transported U.S. Army troops home from Europe after World War I. The ship is commemorated on this "*Souvenir de France*" silk pillow. Printed words include: "The Ship that brought me Home," enclosed in a beribboned, wreath design. Below an image of the ship, a description says: "U.S.S. Leviathan: World's Largest Ship – 950 feet long, 100 feet wide, and 58,000 tons." Other words at the top say, "In memory of my service in France with U.S. Army." The American and French flag poles are crossed and are shown in the upper left quadrant. A brown and gray striped border is present, as well as a short blue fringe. There is a 7" vertical split in the fibers. 15.5" x 16.75". 1918-1919. $45-50.

In September 1918, the same ship transported soldiers home and made a total of nine such journeys to accomplish the task. The *U.S.S. Leviathan* was the largest ship in the Navy until it was surpassed in size by the *Midway*, built in 1945. In September 1919, the *U.S.S. Leviathan* was decommissioned for military use. It saw a few more years of service, but ultimately, it was scrapped for metal components in 1938.[17]

The pillow cover shown here belonged to a soldier named Harvey S. Hilderbrand from Everest, Kansas. He served in the 314th Engineers, 89th Division, and came home from France with a number of souvenirs. Items received with the pillow cover purchase are: 1) A unit history of the 314th Engineers, 2) A troop billet ticket for the *U.S.S. Leviathan*, 3) An unused photo postcard of a doughboy standing next to a wagon that has a sign that says "89th Division," 4) A color postcard of the *U.S.S. Leviathan*, 5) A newspaper clipping about the 89th Division, from an unknown newspaper source, 6) A thirty-three page booklet, "To the Homeward-Bound Americans," and 7) A fold-out

souvenir selection of photos titled, "Aboard the U.S.S. Leviathan," that Hilderbrand signed, in pencil, on the back of one of the photos.

To verify the identity of this soldier, I looked for records at ancestry.com and found a 1920 census record that indicates he was born in 1897 in Missouri. In 1920, he was twenty-three years old and his wife was only twenty years old. At the time of the census, they were living in Pottawatomie, Kansas.

Additional ships besides the *U.S.S. Leviathan* transported troops home from France. Another pillow cover, seen in an eBay auction, has an identical design to this one except that the name of the ship is the *U.S.S. Plattsburg*.

Sketching the Men of War

Gen. John Joseph Pershing

In any consideration of World War I, the name of General John Joseph Pershing (1860-1948) comes up time and again. In the foreword to his book, *My Experiences in the World War, Volume I*, Pershing wrote a tribute to the soldiers whom he commanded:

> The men of all ranks who served with me in France added a brilliant page to the record of the American soldier's devotion to country. This modest work can only outline the stirring narrative of their achievements. No commander was ever privileged to lead a finer force; no commander ever derived greater inspiration from the performance of his troops.

Two sketches of Pershing can be viewed in *The World's Work* magazine, April 1919, in an article written and illustrated by Joseph Cummings Chase (1878-1965), "Corporal York, General Pershing, and Others." A trained artist, Chase was commissioned to create official portraits of generals, presidents, and other important people in society. Chase would later write a book, *Face Value: Autobiography of The Portrait Painter* (New York: Rolton House Inc., Publishers, 1962). The National Gallery of Art has collected many of Chase's portraits.

Two completely different demeanors of Pershing were captured by Chase in the sketches shown in his article. One of them shows a troubled man, deeply concerned about winning the war, while a second drawing shows a calm, dignified man who exhibits a sense of relief when the war was essentially over, after the American Army occupied part of Germany. Keep in mind that the "Victory Parade" in Paris was held on July 14, 1919.

Cpl. Alvin C. York: Instant Hero

Chase, a career artist, is responsible for a number of art designs published as covers for *The Saturday Evening Post*. Chase was surprised when asked to do a field sketch of the now famous U.S. Army Corporal Alvin C. York, a member of Company G, 328th Infantry. York, an enlisted soldier, opposed the war at first on the grounds of being a "conscientious objector." After a change of heart, he joined the Army and distinguished himself by killing twenty Germans and capturing 132 German prisoners in one day. He achieved this feat almost single-handedly, with only seven remaining men of his unit available for backup. The details of the fight were provided by George Patullo, who broke the story in *The Saturday Evening Post* on April 26, 1919, in an article titled, "The Second Elder Gives Battle." A movie was made about York's life and a book published about him titled, *Sgt. York: His Life, Legend & Legacy* by John Perry.

On this silk U.S. Army pillow cover, the American flag with forty-eight stars waves proudly over the word "Mother" in large, shadowed letters. In the lower right corner, a group of doughboys are marching. The overlaid words are "Our Infantry." The background of this silk item is enhanced with pastel hues in mint green, pink, yellow, and blue and the 4" green fringe gives a dramatic effect. 16.125" x 16.125". 1917-1918. $45-50.

"U.S. Field Artillery" is the name that is satin-stitched by machine onto this light-brown, felted wool, pillow cover from World War I. In the center are two crossed cannons. Moth damage consists of only a few tiny holes. 17.125" x 17.125". 1917-1918. $20-25.

This charming U.S. Army silk pillow cover shows "Uncle Sam" saying "Good Bye, Good Luck, God Bless You!" to General John Joseph Pershing, as troops march by in formation carrying flags and a biplane passes overhead. 16.125" x 16". 1917-1918. $35-45.

Felted wool appliqué embellish this U.S. Army felted wool pillow cover. The only exception is an American flag in silk. The words "War 1917" and the large white letters "U.S.A.," as well as a large thread-painted eagle, appear on this patriotic pillow in red, white, and blue. A bright pink grosgrain ribbon is folded in half and is interlaced through slits to join the back and the front of the pillow cover together. The outer, simulated, fringed edges have been achieved by cutting the felted wool in angular strips all around. 21.125" x 12.125". 1917. $25-35.

Chapter Three

Civilian Conservation Camps
& their Souvenir Pillow Covers

Author's Note: In this chapter and for the rest of the book, there will be no mention of the color of fringes or their measurements unless the fringe is a rare color or is exceptionally long or short.

The financial crash of 1929 on Wall Street plunged the country into a panic. By the time President Herbert Clark Hoover (1874-1964) sought re-election in 1932 on the Republican ticket, the unemployment rate was more than twenty-five percent, food was scarce, and America resembled a Third World Country, as people stood in long lines to collect meager portions of soup and bread. In addition, parts of the country were experiencing a major drought, as is well documented in the songs of folksinger, Woody Guthrie (1912-1967).

Franklin Delano Roosevelt (1882-1945), a Democrat, promised the country a "New Deal" and ways "to restore America to its own people." He promised to create much needed jobs. Once elected, he kept his campaign promises very quickly. With the cooperation of Congress, he established the Civilian Conservation Corps within just thirty-seven days of taking office.

Roosevelt realized that the excessive, clear-cutting of timber that had occurred in the 1920s and 1930s had eroded the topsoil and caused flooding. To stabilize the land, he engaged unemployed young men (ages 18 to 26) in a tree-planting program. Even though they were clearly outside the parameter of the age guidelines, veterans from World War I could join the C.C.C. and, as a result, 25,000 veterans seized the opportunity. Blacks were accepted into integrated units of the C.C.C., but soon were placed in segregated units except for their white officers. In all, 1-1/3 billion trees were planted.

The Civilian Conservation Corps asked recruits to stay for six months. That turned out to be no problem! The organization was in place from 1933 to 1942, sometimes referred to as "Roosevelt's Tree Army." However, that terminology incurred the ire of those who did not like the word "Army," as it reminded them of the private armies of Mussolini and Hitler (the SA, a forerunner of the SS). In fact, for his very effective efforts at aiding the economy, Roosevelt was called a "Socialist" and even a "Communist" by his detractors.

This bronze statue of a young man holding an axe stands at present-day Bear Brook State Park in Allenstown, New Hampshire, a site built by members of the Civilian Conservation Corps. The inscription, titled "The C.C.C. Worker," says: "*This statue is dedicated to the young men who served in the Civilian Conservation Corps from 1933 to 1942. Their work in the parks and forests of New Hampshire can be enjoyed today. Dedicated September 29, 2001 by the New Hampshire Chapter 107 - CCC Alumni, Department of Resources and Economic Development and the Department of Cultural Resources.*"

If you have ever visited a state or national park, chances are good that C.C.C. workers had a part in its construction. Every state in The Union hosted C.C.C. units, as did the territories of Alaska and Hawaii, the U.S. Virgin Islands, and Puerto Rico. In Allenstown, New Hampshire, just five miles from my childhood home, is Bear Brook State Park, where I swam often as a child. The three ponds within the park were totally excavated by C.C.C. workers, who also hauled large slabs of granite rock from Hooksett, New Hampshire, to build the bathhouse on the public beach there.

Life in a Civilian Conservation Camp

The Civilian Conservation Corps was run like the military and exceeded the role of only providing work. Hearty meals, hard work, fresh air, discipline, and recreational and educational activities improved the health and minds of the men. They worked six hours a day, but later had time for enjoyable activities and camaraderie. The organization was instrumental in helping to lift a suffering nation out of the Great Depression. By 1942, when Congress did not pass legislation to again fund C.C.C. activities, the men who had undergone training there were pre-trained candidates for the military. Many signed up for the Army to fight in World War II.

From his C.C.C. camp in Priest River, Idaho, a young man named John Grabania sent his mother this pretty pillow cover. One could request that pillows be personalized with their name or other additional information, as seen on this textile. At the time, his parents, Joseph and Eva, lived in North Charleroni, Pennsylvania, with their seven other children. Online records indicate that John later joined the U.S. Army on August 5, 1943, for the duration of World War II plus six months.

This overwhelmingly pink Civilian Conservation Corps pillow is personalized with the name "John Grabania," a member of "Company #1501 C.C.C.," Priest River, Idaho. The rayon cloth has an unusual weave that is not usually seen on these types of pillows. The background is printed with roses, a cottage scene, and a poem for "Mother": "To one who bears the sweetest name / and adds a lustre [sic] to the same [...]." 16.75" x 15.25". 1933-1942. $20-30.

For Mr. Grabania and the 3-1/3 million other men who served in the U.S. Civilian Conservation Corps (1933-1942), there was perhaps no more endearing an object to purchase in the canteen than a "Mother" pillow cover. Sentiment for "Mother" and home was waxing high in those unfamiliar days of being away from home, probably for the first time, and being subject to military style rules.

Alderic O. "Dick" Violette: A Leader and Soldier

Several years ago, we had the opportunity to meet Alderic O. "Dick" Violette, a man who served at C.C.C. Camp #1147 in Warner, New Hampshire. Like many others who served in the Civilian Conservation Corps, he was called to join in the U.S. Army during World War II. He was a member of the 129th Infantry Division in the Philippines. He fondly remembers his days in the C.C.C. and recalls the pranks pulled by some of the young men. He compares their antics to those of college fraternity members. For example, the men would move around the personal belongings of others just to create confusion. They would even place beds atop flagpoles. (Do not ask me how that was done!). "Most of the actions were in good fun," he states.

An anecdote in the book, *Builder of Men: Life in C.C.C. Camps of New Hampshire* by David D. Draves, mentions the unfortunate situation of a young man who was found alone in the C.C.C. barracks when he was supposed to be painting the Mess Hall. He was caught red-handed with stolen chocolates and "Mother" pillows right before Mother's Day. He'd learned to pick trunk locks and had helped himself to the personal belongings of others.[1]

The Commanding Officer decided not to dismiss the young man, but make him stay, thinking that punishment would be meted out by his peers. His thought was correct. In Drave's book, Violette is quoted as saying: "I've seen 'im with a couple of black eyes, lumps on his face. They pounded 'im. But that young fellow, before I left camp, was an assistant leader."[2]

The C.C.C. published a weekly paper called *Happy Days Newspaper* in which they offered "pillow shams" sold by the Brinker Supply Company of Steubenville, Ohio ("the headquarters for C.C.C. pillows," as well as the Western Art Leather Co. of Denver, Colorado. The Brinker Company offered nine different designs on fine "satin" (actually rayon with a "satin" weave). Types of pillows that could be ordered were: "1) Mother, 2) Mother and Dad, 3) Sweetheart, 4) Sister, 5) Friendship, 6) Wife, 7) Forget Me Not, 8) Special C.C.C. Souvenir Design, and 9) N.Y. World's Fair Designs." All cost $1 dollar each, postpaid. A copy of the ad can be viewed online at the Broward County Library site.[3]

Featuring a surveyor, a plantation of trees planted by the "Tree Army," and landscape scenes, this C.C.C. pillow cover features a poem to "Sister": "Of all the Girls / I ever knew, / There never was / One like you / You're the nearest / You're the dearest / Pal I ever knew." This poem frequently shows up on pillow covers from 1933 to 1945. This item is in excellent condition. 16.125" x 16.125". $25-40.

The Western Art Leather Company sold 20" x 20" "satin" pillows that were fringed. They, too, offered various designations. The bulk cost was $6.25 per dozen, postpaid; or quality 18" x 18" sateen pillows for $3.75 per dozen. As you can see, if the C.C.C. camps were selling them to group members at $1 dollar each, the revenue would have been between forty-eight cents and seventy-one cents per pillow cover.

I have had the personal pleasure of hearing two people sing the "Mother" song, both of whom lived during the war years of World War II. This song tribute to "Mother" has the same first verse of a poem to "Mother" that is printed on C.C.C. and World War II pillow covers.

"M-O-T-H-E-R (A Word that Means The World To Me)" is a song written by Howard Johnson (lyrics) and Theodore Morse (music). The finished song was copyrighted in 1915 by Leo Feist, Inc., 1619 Broadway, New York, New York. The one-page of sheet music is included in a short compilation of songs titled, "Bill Hardey's Songs of the Gay Nineties and Other Old Favorites," published by Robbins Music Corporation, 799 Seventh Avenue, New York City, a company that is now out of business.

The song has two verses, the first of which is the one printed on the pillow covers. The second verse says: "M is for the mercy she possesses / O means that I owe her all I own, / T is for the tender sweet caresses / H is for her hands that made a home, / E means ev'rything she's done to help me / R means real and regular, you see, / Put them all together, they spell, "MOTHER," / A word that means the world to me."

This is a very special C.C.C. pillow for a number of reasons. Made by GEMSCO, New York, it has a background fabric (type unknown) that may be de-lustered rayon textured in an interesting chevron pattern. A sketch of "mother" is featured, as well as a "Mother" poem: "M is for the million things she gave me / O means only that she's growing old / T is for the tears she shed to save me / H is for her heart of purest gold / E is for her eyes with love light shining / R means right and right she'll always be / Put them all together they spell / MOTHER / A word that means the world to me." 16" x 16". 1933-1942. In spite of its used condition, and an issue with the left top fringe, this pillow cover is unusual enough to warrant a value of $30-40. *Courtesy of Lyell D. Henry.*

This is a scan of vintage sheet music for the song titled "M-O-T-H-E-R," whose lyrics are
repeated on many Civilian Conservation Corps and World War II pillow covers.

The men of the C.C.C. became strong through hard work, exercise, and good food. Alderic O. "Dick" Violette provided us with a menu for the Thanksgiving meal served in 1936 to members of his C.C.C. camp, the 1147th Company, Warner Camp Number 11016. The men enjoyed English Turkey Soup, celery, stuffed olives, mixed pickles, roast turkey, nut dressing, snowflake potatoes, candied sweet potatoes, giblet gravy, mashed turnips, cranberry sauce, lettuce and tomato salad, Parker House rolls, butter, mince pie, pumpkin pie, ice cream, oranges, grapes, assorted nuts, mixed candy, figs, pimentos [sic], salted peanuts, cherries, coffee, and cigarettes (before the awareness that they are not healthy).

President Franklin D. Roosevelt's plan to rebuild the country by using its untapped resources, namely, young men and the environment, had far-reaching and lasting benefits. However, in addition to providing for the temporal needs of those involved in the Civilian Conservation Corps, the organization's work brought to light the idea that all Americans should carefully guard the land and natural resources.

The Civilian Conservation Corps logo and the large lime green letters "C.C.C.," shadowed in gray, are integral components of this acetate pillow cover that features a poem to "Mother and Dad": "No one know but Mother and Dad / About the smiles and tears we've had [...]." The overall graphic quality of this pillow cover makes it special, with its large eagle, flags, and scenes of camp life. 16.125" x 16.75". 1933-1942. $12-20.

The most charming feature of this item is its symbol of a tree within a triangle and the capital letter "C" placed in each corner to represent the Civilian Conservation Corps. With an ochre background, there are two lovely roses that look hand-painted. The usual "Mother and Dad" poem has amended words: "In all the years I've / known you both ~ / You planned and strived for me. / Through sacrifice of / everything / That could a pleasure be / This cluster of roses I'm / sending, / Just as a thought from me." The predominantly blue fringe is a remarkably long length at 3.125". This textile is in excellent condition. 16.125" x 16.625". 1933-1942. $24-30.

This rayon C.C.C. pillow cover, made in a satin weave, is from Company #1123 in New Hampshire. Its "Sweetheart" poem says, "I thought that you would / like to know / that someone's thoughts go / where you go [...]." The camp setting scene is accompanied by two flags, an eagle, roses, and the C.C.C. insignia. This item and the next two pillow covers belong to a museum exhibit and were not measured. The date range is 1933-1942 for all of them. *Courtesy of Alderic O. "Dick" Violette.*

This rayon pillow cover with a light turquoise background is from Company #130 in New Hampshire. Design motifs include an eagle with a shield whose talons are grasping arrows, and olive branches. The "Mother" poem says, "There's a dear little house inviting / in a dear little place I know [...]." *Courtesy of Alderic O. "Dick" Violette.*

This rayon pillow cover says, "Souvenir of U.S.A., Civilian Conservation Corps, Company #130." Its named scenes include: 1) "Fighting Forest Fires," 2) "Study," 3) "Building," 4) "Boxing," 5) "Music," and "Sports." *Courtesy of Alderic O. "Dick" Violette.*

Chapter Four

U.S. Army
Pillow Covers of World War II

Textiles as Expression of Patriotism, Sentiment, and Points of Connection

World War II pillow covers are artifacts that can have a wide range of condition issues today as well as a broad range of prices. When someone sees a pillow cover with a price of ninety-nine cents, it could mean that there is something very wrong with the textile, or perhaps the seller just wants "to get rid of" an item online because it has not sold in a shop. When I began collecting pillow covers a few years ago, the auctions were starting at $4.99. Today, most auctions have a starting bid of at least $9.99 or $19.99. Recently, those beginning bids have increased even more, to as much as $39.99 or $49.99.

A couple of years ago, a young man sent me a photo of his grandmother's pillow cover and suggested that he would not sell it for less than $200. At the time, it seemed that this grandson was not really ready to give up his piece of family history. It is impossible to recoup the sentimental value of an object. Lately, many buy-it-now auctions on eBay have high price tags attached, as much as $400 or even $800 for pillow covers touted to be "rare." Online auctions are the great equalizer and soon reveal whether an item is "rare" or not.

If you have a pillow cover for sale, please describe it adequately. As a quick point of reference, virtually none of the pillow covers were silk during World War II. Consumers are misled by rayon because it can be manufactured to mimic "cotton, linen, wool, and [or] silk."[1] Since the type of fibers in a textile will dictate the proper care of that item, the importance of misrepresentation cannot be overstated. Tips on proper care are provided in Chapter Nine.

"The Stars and Stripes Forever" slogan is featured on this "Mother" pillow cover sent from Fort Sill, Oklahoma. Its poem says: "To one who bears the sweetest name / And adds a luster to the same. […]." This item is in mint condition. 16.75" x 17". 1941-1945. $10-20.

A huge American flag graces the surface of this Fort Sill, Oklahoma, U.S. Army pillow cover. When it was founded in 1869, the site was called Camp Wichita. Major General Philip H. Sheridan (1831-1888) renamed the camp to honor his fallen colleague, Union Brigadier General Joshua W. Sill (1831-1862) who was killed at the Battle of Stones River, Tennessee, during the American Civil War. The camp was built during the Indian Wars and is the only remaining active Army fort from that time period still used today. Fort Sill was designated a national monument in 1960.[2]

Fort Benning, Georgia, was originally set up in 1918 as Camp Benning and named in honor of a Confederate General, Henry Lewis Benning (1814-1875). During World War I, the site, which is located in Georgia, with only seven percent of its land area in Tennessee, served as a combat training center. During the 1930s, the Civilian Conservation Corps built all of the permanent wooden buildings still in use today.

The 555th Parachute Infantry trained at this Fort to learn to be "smoke jumpers" or to fight fires. The 2nd Armored Division, which saw action in the Pacific Theater during World War II, also trained at Fort Benning. During the Vietnam War, scout dogs received training there in how to detect enemy ambushes.[3]

The insignia of the 99th U.S. Army Infantry division features the color black to symbolize the iron of the mills of Pittsburg, Pennsylvania, the hometown of many of its members. The superimposed grid of blue and white squares takes it coloration from the Coat of Arms design that belongs to the family of William Pitt[4], the man for whom Pittsburg was named.[5]

The 99th Infantry, an active unit of World War II, distinguished itself during the Battle of the Bulge by fiercely fighting off the German Sixth Panzer Army and blocking the soldiers from overtaking the roads that led to Belgium. The Intelligence and Reconnaissance Platoon of the 394th Infantry Regiment of this Division is the most highly decorated platoon of WWII.[6]

Two armed soldiers are viewing an eagle that is positioned under the words "U.S. Army." This pillow cover, marked "Fort Benning, Georgia," has the following "Mother" poem: "A mother sweet and dear as you / Is such a rare delight / Because your loving thoughtful ways / Make Life more fine and bright / You share when I am sad or glad / The dearest one I ever had!" There is a tiny stain on the front and the pillow backing fabric has long linear splits. 16.125" x 16.375". 1941-1945. $5-10.

This World War II pillow cover has a "Mother" poem: "With spirit calm as the / summer sea / Moving in sweet serenity / I am sure there is no other / In all the world like you / My Mother." This textile features the shield insignia design of the U.S. Army's 99th Infantry. This is in mint condition. 17" x 17". 1941-1945. $20-30.

In June 1941, Fort Stewart, Georgia, was renamed Camp Stewart and set up as an anti-aircraft artillery center that was very active during World War II. During that time, the Women's Air Force Service Pilots (WASP unit) was located at the site. Named for an American Revolutionary War hero, General Daniel Stewart (1761-1829), the Camp held Italian and German prisoners of war from 1943-1945.[7]

"To My Wife" is the featured poem on this U.S. Army blue and yellow pillow cover from Camp Stewart, Georgia. All flocked letters are capitalized and read: "A darling little wife / has made my dreams come true / she blesses all my life / her name is only you / You are my partner sweet / you share in all I do / and make my joy complete / by simply being you." The mangled fringe gives it a lesser value. 16.5" x 17.5". 1941-1945. $5-10.

A Personal Connection to Fort Bragg

Inserted in the pocket of this rayon, U.S. Army pillow cover from Fort Bragg, North Carolina, is a Christmas card sent from Europe in 1944 that shows the "V" for Victory design.

Founded in 1918 and finished in 1919, Fort Bragg, North Carolina, was formerly called Camp Bragg, named for Confederate Army General Braxton Bragg (1817-1876). Its original mission was to train soldiers in the use of field artillery. After World War I, the site was in danger of being closed, but in 1922 it achieved permanent status as a U.S. Army base and was renamed Fort Bragg at that time. Over the years its mission has changed.[8]

This photo, taken on March 9, 1941, shows my uncle, Martin A. Fischer, standing between his mother (my grandmother), Nancy Lynam Fischer, on the left, and his eldest sister (my aunt), Frances Fischer, on the right. He enlisted in the Army on February 24, 1941, at the age of seventeen, concealing his true age like many other young men who were "gung ho" to fight in World War II. On March 19, 1944, the day he left for Fort Dix and subsequent deployment to the European front, Nancy Fischer died of a cerebral hemorrhage. At just fifty-two years old, and with ten other children, she can be considered a casualty of war on the home front. He never had the chance to send her mail of any kind, let alone a "Sweetheart-Mother" pillow.

In the photo insertion pocket of this pillow cover, I have placed a 1944 postcard with a "V" for Victory design. This was sent to my mother, Elizabeth Grace (and her family), as a Christmas greeting card from "Somewhere in Germany" from Martin A. Fischer, her younger brother who was serving in the U.S. Army. There is a hand-written message on the back of the card. The red, white, and blue motifs, including a bird, lend a patriotic air to this textile. Some migration of color is visible on the white background. A poem for "Mother" says: "This picture, Mother / just for you / brings my love / all year through." 16" x 16". 1941-1945. $10-15.

Fort Belvoir, Virginia, was previously the residence of William Fairfax before becoming host to many different U.S. Army units. The castle insignia has been the symbol of the Army Corps of Engineers since 1902. The 249th Engineer Battalion calls this military installation "home."[9]

This very "busy," colorful pillow cover, with scenes of soldiers in action and yellow roses, features a half-circle banner that lists all U.S. Army units and their insignia. Listed are: 1) "Air Force," 2) "Coast Artillery," 3) "Quartermaster," 4) "Armored Force," 5) "Field Artillery," 6) "Parachutists," 7) "Infantry," 8) "Cavalry," 9) "Medical Corps," 10) "Signal Corps," 11) "Engineers," 12) "Chemical Warfare," 14) "Military Police," and 15) "Ordinance."

The following "Sweetheart" poem appears on a yellow and blue, rayon pillow cover from the U.S. Army at Fort Belvoir, Virginia: "I thought that you / would like to know / That someone's thoughts / go where you go; / That someone / never can forget / The hours we spent since first we met. / That life is richer / sweeter far, / for such a sweetheart / as you are. / And now my constant prayer / will be / That God may keep you / safe for me." 17" x 17". 1941-1945. $10-15.

The following friendship poem is included on a rayon pillow cover that says "U.S. Army" and "Los Angeles, California": "Wishing there were / More like you, / I meet a lot of people / In my travels every day / Congenial friends, and cordial ones / And fine in every way / And though I'm very fond of them / And deem them charming too, / I just can't keep from wishing / There were more of them like you." 16.875" x 17.375". 1943-1945. $5-15.

Some pillow covers feature no poetry or designation of specific location. This rayon U.S. Army pillow, "To My Sweetheart," displays an elongated flag and a ribbon banner that repeats the name, "U.S. Army." The pillow cover is predominantly red, white, and blue. A spray of roses is the main motif. The pillow has diminished value, with its red flocking showing considerable wear and tear from being leaned on (as a pillow). 16.375" x 16". 1941-1945. $6-10.

On this rayon U.S. Army pillow cover, an angry Grizzly Bear hurls bombs toward the Aleutian Islands from Alaska. He was directing them toward the Japanese who began occupying the two islands of Attu and Kiska on June 3, 1942. Due to the remote location of the islands, the Japanese were not ousted for one year. Their plan was to block a U.S. invasion from the Northern Pacific. This is a very desirable pillow cover, based on its cartoon-like image of the bear and the history it represents. The yellow and red flocking colors are set off nicely by a fringe of the same two colors. The back of this pillow is a cotton fabric with large white stars on a blue background. 16.875" x 16.375". 1941-1945. $50-60.

In January 1942, three hundred local families were displaced to clear the way for a Tank Destroyer Tactical and Training Center, which eventually became Fort Hood in Texas. At its peak population, the number of soldiers there reached 95,000 men in June 1943. By the following year, the mission was changed and Field Artillery battalions predominated, along with an Infantry Replacement Center. The site is still operational.

On November 5, 2009, Major Nidal Malik Hassan, a psychiatrist, shot thirteen fellow Army personnel to death and wounded thirty others.[10] He is an American born Muslim whose family roots are in Palestine. The media suggested that Hassan has radical Islam beliefs. He was shot at the time of the incident and is now paralyzed.

The named scenes on this U.S. Army "Mother" pillow from Fort Hood, Texas, are listed as 1) "Helicopter," 2) "Howitzer Crew," 3) "U.S. Army Tank," 4) "On the Rifle Range," 5) "Mortar Crew," and 6) "Preparing a Missile." The poem is the same one that is oft repeated: "To one who bears / the sweetest name / And adds a luster / to the same [...]." This textile has nice color contrast and is in very good condition (never used). 15.875" x 16.875". Circa 1960s-early 1970s. $10-20.

Camp Wheeler, Georgia, was named for Confederate General Joseph Wheeler (1836-1906). This U.S. Army training camp was established during World War I, from 1917 to 1919, and was reopened during World War II as an Infantry Replacement Center from 1940 to 1946. The focus at that time was training soldiers in the handling of small arms. One of its units was the 7th Infantry Division. The site was constructed on leased land and held German prisoners of war.[11]

The "Mother" poem featured on this pillow cover is based on a charming quote attributed to Abraham Lincoln. The sentiment is made more poignant when we realize that Lincoln lost his mother at any early age. Nancy Hanks Lincoln (1784-1818) died from "milk sickness" when "Abe" was only nine years old. That illness comes about after one has consumed the

This rayon "Mother" pillow cover from Camp Wheeler, Georgia, is very unusual as it has flocked images and words in nearly the same medium orange color. This makes the designs difficult to see, unless one is in close proximity. Even more startling is the contrasting green fringe embellished with yellow rayon yarn. The words say: "All that I am, or hope / to be, I owe to my / angel mother. *Lincoln.*" A similar, monochromatic, U.S. Coast Guard pillow cover with this same poem was featured in an online auction. 16" x 16.625". 1941-1945. $20-30.

milk of a cow that has ingested poisonous snakeroot. Mrs. Lincoln and her husband, Thomas, whom she married in 1806, had three children: Sarah (1807); Abraham (1809); and Thomas (1812), who died as an infant.[12]

This particular pillow cover has a lot of surface damage to its flocked letters and designs. Yet, it is still here to remind us of Camp Blanding, Florida. Built in 1940, more than 800,000 troops were trained at the site during World War II. The camp served as a departure point for soldiers deploying overseas. Since the end of the war, Camp Blanding has undergone many changes. Today, it is an active military installation that hosts the National Guard.[13]

The flocked designs and lettering of this rayon pillow cover celebrate Camp Blanding, Florida, named in honor of Florida's distinguished Lieutenant Colonel Albert H. Blanding (1876-1970). 17" x 17.25". 1940-1945. $10-15.

Camp Maxey, Texas, opened on July 15, 1942, and was named for Confederate General Samuel Bell Maxey (1825-1895). Set up as an infantry training site, it was home to the 102nd Infantry Division and the 793rd Military Police, a battalion that spent time in Scotland in 1944 to prepare for the invasion of France. After World War II, the site was deactivated on October 1, 1945.[14]

This striking "V" for Victory pillow cover, in red and blue on a yellow rayon background, represents a U.S. Army site that was short-lived, Camp Maxey, Texas. 16.25" x 16.75". 1942-1945. $13-20.

Fort Leonard Wood, Missouri, has earned the amusing moniker of "Fort Lost in the Woods" because of its location in the Ozark Mountains, an area with variable weather. Established in 1940, with the intent of making it an infantry training site, in 1941 it was named for General Leonard Wood (1860-1927).[15] The base was repurposed as an Engineer Replacement Training Center. Although now used for other purposes, the military site is still operational.[16]

Camp Hood, Texas, was named in honor of Confederate General John Bell Hood (1831-1879).[18] This World War II pillow cover features an eagle that is superimposed on a "V" for "Victory" letter. At the top opening of the "V" is a tiger, enclosed within a circle. The words "Seek, Strike, Destroy" appear within the circle. The roses (for Mother) are a charming part of the surface design. Offset by a bright, ochre color fringe, this textile is visually dynamic.

This cover from Fort Leonard Wood, Missouri, has a tag that says, "100% acetate, exclusive of decoration." An eagle, roses, and a poem for "Grandmother" grace the pillow cover. The word "Grandmother" is substituted for a poem that usually is for "Mother": "To one who bears / the sweetest name / And adds a luster / to the same [...]." 15.875" x 15.625". 1940-1945. $10-20.

The bright, ochre color flocked decorations and fringe of this green, acetate, pillow cover from Fort Leonard Wood, Missouri, are visually striking. Its poem says, "Mother": "With spirit calm as the / summer sea / Moving in sweet serenity [...]." 16.75" x 17". 1940-1945. $20-25.

The poem on this rayon, U.S. Army "Mother" pillow cover from Camp Hood, Texas, says: "There are millions of leaves / on the trees, dear Mom ~ / Millions of stars up above ~ / Millions of mothers all / over the world, / But just one dear Mom I love." 16.625" x 17.5". 1942-1945. $20-30.

This pillow cover may have been sold during World War II or the Korean War. Camp Stoneman in Pittsburg, California, was active as a staging area for the U.S. Army from 1942 to 1954 when it was decommissioned.[17]

This "Sweetheart" U.S. Army pillow from Camp Stoneman, California, has a pretty, rust color background with gray motifs and yellow flocked letters. The fabric *may be* acetate. The poem says: "A picture, a letter, a word / from you – And suddenly all / of my dreams come true, / You're close in my arms / and I hold you tight, / I feel your soft kiss as you / Whisper, 'Good Night'." This item is in very good condition. 16.875" x 17.875". 1942-1954. $10-20.

Fort Totten was named in honor of Joseph Gilbert Totten (1788-1864),[19] a graduate of West Point and a member of the U.S. Army Corps of Engineers during the War of 1812. The old fort, built in 1898, was used again during World War II. Situated on a peninsula located on the north shore of Long Island, New York, the fort was built to protect the East River that has an access point to New York Harbor.

The fort was closed as an active military site in 1974 and many of the former Army buildings are in disrepair. The property was purchased by the City of New York Parks and Recreation Department, which maintains a portion of it as a public park. Headquarters of the Bayside Historical Society are located here and the Army Reserve also maintains "a presence."[20]

Fort Monmouth, New Jersey, was not established as a permanent U.S. Army base until 1925. At that time, it was named in honor of all who died at the Battle of Monmouth during the American Revolutionary War. During World War II, the Signal Corps Officer Training School was predominant in site activities. "A radio-based aircraft detection system,"[21] was developed at the base. This radar system was used by two U.S. Army privates, Elliot and Joseph Lockard, at Opana Point, Hawaii. They detected the incoming formation of Japanese war planes on December 7, 1941, ten hours before they struck Pearl Harbor, but their reports were discounted and unheeded by those in charge, with devastating results.

Blue planes form a "V" for "Victory" sign on this very graphic U.S. Army pillow cover from Fort Totten, New York. The addition of a yellow fringe, setting off the blue and red colors on the main part of the cover, completes a classic triadic color combination. The abbreviations "A.A.A.C., E.D.C." appear within the "V." 16.25" x 17.625". 1941-1945. $30-40.

Named scenes on this U.S. Army pillow cover from Fort Monmouth, New Jersey, include: 1) "Machine Gunner," 2) "Tanks," 3) "Artillery in Action," 4) "Infantry Attack," and 5) "Anti-Aircraft." A banner at the top says: "Defenders of Our Liberty." This wonderful gift from an online vendor is in excellent condition! 16.125" x 17.125". 1941-1945. *Courtesy of "Walt."*

Fort George G. Meade, located in Maryland and named for Civil War Union General George Gordon Meade (1815-1872),[22] was initially established as Camp Annapolis Junction in 1917. Later, it was called Camp Admiral, and for a short time, Fort Leonard Wood. During the 1930s, it was again called Fort George G. Meade. During World War II, the camp held prisoners of war, and served to train soldiers in basic training.[23]

Just months after the attack on Pearl Harbor in 1941, Camp Atterbury in Indiana was constructed and would be the training site of four U.S. Army divisions including the 30th, 83rd, 92nd, and 106th divisions, as well as the 39th Evacuation Hospital. The 106th division sustained major casualties at the Battle of the Bulge, the final major battle of World War II. German and Italian prisoners of war were held at the camp. The Wakeman General and Convalescent Hospital was the largest of its kind with forty-seven buildings. The site went out of active use in 1946. Since 2001, the Indiana National Guard has used the area as a training site.[24]

This Fort George G. Meade pillow cover features four scenes of Army equipment and three pink roses. Its "Sweetheart" poem says: "Love unending, warm and true / Sweetheart mine, this brings to you / Love which hopes that Happiness / All your days may Cheer and Bless." The original sale price tag, added at the military base, is stapled to the upper left corner: "$7.50," or "$7.80 with envelope". 16.375" x 16.875". 1941-1945. $30-40.

This U.S. Army pillow cover from Camp Atterbury, Indiana, is the first military pillow I ever collected! Its endearing poem and large spray of roses caught my attention: "Sweetheart," "Just for yourself I love you / for the things you do / For your sunny smile and happy ways / Your heart that's always True / Some win their way with favors / or treasures they may own / But you are dear to me Sweetheart / for your Dear Self alone." 16.125" x 16.375". 1941-1945. $20-30.

The second of these two photos shows an envelope that contains a "boudoir" pillow cover that was never mailed or opened. One can only speculate as to the reason it was not sent. The bottom of the envelope has the words "Satin Rayon ~ Ready to Fill." While the word "satin," as a descriptor for rayon, may add a sense of aesthetic value or imply that the product is composed of luxury fibers, the inclusion of that word is actually non-functional. Satin is a type of weave and does not refer to a particular fabric.

The term "satin" originated in Zaytun, China. The first cloth woven in a satin weave was produced in eleventh century Italy. By the fourteenth century, "satin" cloth was available in England. Silk, nylon, or polyester fibers can be woven in a satin weave. When cotton is present, the cloth is referred to as "cotton sateen."[25]

Boudoir quilts, with their soft, lustrous surfaces, were popular textiles that were sold beginning in the late 1920s. Manufactured in solid colors (not prints), the only decoration on their whole cloth surfaces were the quilting stitches themselves.

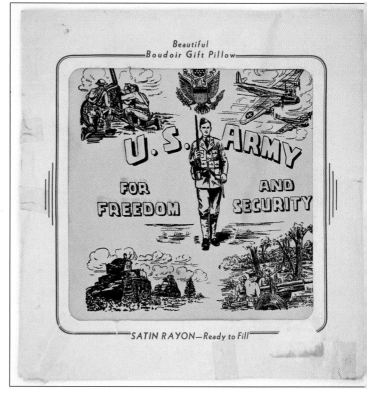

A similar U.S. Army pillow cover, in a different color, features the words "For Freedom and Security" seen through the window of the original envelope in which it was sold. Advertised as a "beautiful, boudoir, gift pillow" in "satin rayon" and "ready to fill," this pillow cover has a light orange background and blue printed images. The amount of postage required to mail this item at the time is printed on the back in the upper right corner: "1-1/2 c." Three-cent stamps were issued in 1938 with the image of Benjamin Franklin on them and were in use throughout the 1940s, according to the postage stamp guide at about.com. It was fun to collect this pillow cover in its original envelope that was never mailed. The actual textile has never been removed from the package. The envelope's size is 11.125" x 11.75". 1941-1945. $26-40.

"For Freedom and Security" appear on this generic U.S. Army pillow cover. Six scenes are shown, two of them named "Field Artillery" and "Anti-Aircraft Artillery." A soldier in uniform stands besides a poem: "To My Wife." It reads: "Memories' garden I recall / The sweetheart days we knew / With lovely flowers, singing birds / And skies of azure blue. / Dear Wife of Mine how / sweet the words / A hoped for dream come true, / My heart is happy when / I think / Of home sweet home, and You." The background is light tan and all of the images are printed in blue ink. Excellent condition. 15.625" x 16.625". 1941-1945. $20-30.

Camp Kohler, a Signal Corps training center located north of Sacramento, California was set up in 1942 and named for Lieutenant Frederick L. Kohler, an officer who was killed in China that same year. During World War II, one of the site's functions was to hold 590 prisoners of war, most of them Japanese American citizens. On March 1, 1946, the camp was discontinued as a Signal Corps training center. On June 20, 1947, most of the camp was destroyed by fire.[26]

Built hurriedly as a Mobilization Training Replacement Center during World War II, Camp Croft, South Carolina, was an active military site from 1941 to 1946. In addition to regular personnel, including members of the Women's Army Corps (WAC), the camp held German prisoners of war. One of the soldiers who trained at Camp Croft was Henry Kissinger. In fact, he became a naturalized citizen while there. Before shutting down altogether at the end of the war, Camp Croft served as the location from which many soldiers were discharged.[27]

Camp Livingston, Louisiana, was first called Camp Tioga. This U.S. Army military site was renamed in honor of the person who negotiated the Louisiana Purchase, Chancellor Robert R. Livingston (1746-1813). It was an active training location from 1940 to 1945 and more than one million troops, members of many different divisions and battalions, were stationed there. Most notable were the "Avengers of Bataan" (the 38th Division); and the first unit to enter Germany by crossing the Danube River (the 86th Division). Now managed by the U.S. Forest Service, the former base is a part of the Kitsachie National Forest.[28]

This rayon U.S. Army Signal Corps pillow cover from Camp Kohler, California, features their insignia, a prominent red, white, and blue design that takes center stage. The design elements are flocked. 16.375" x 16.375". 1941-1945. $15-20.

This rayon U.S. Army pillow cover from Camp Croft, South Carolina, features four named scenes: 1) "Parade Rest," 2) "Field Artillery in Action," 3) "Field Artillery Gun and Crew," and 4) "Anti-Aircraft Gun and Crew." An American eagle oversees the entire operation. An oft-seen "Sweetheart" poem begins, "I thought that you would like to know / That someone's thoughts go where you go: [...]." 16.375" x 16.75". 1941-1946. $20-25.

This rayon U.S. Army pillow cover, from Camp Livingston, Louisiana, has great contrast of color, making the designs easy to see. The scenes are the same ones seen on the previous pillow cover image. A "Mother" poem reads: "There's a dear little house inviting / In a dear little place I know, / And a welcome is always waiting, / When to that little house I go. / For their lives the dearest lady / The sweetest I ever met. / And to-day, if I cannot visit, / Dear Mother, I don't forget." 16.5" x 16.75". 1941-1945. $20-25.

Fort Dix, formerly called Camp Dix, was named for Major General John Adams Dix (1798-1879), who fought in the War of 1812 and as a Union general in the American Civil War. The Camp/Fort was used for the same purpose during World War I as in World War II: as a training and staging area, and after the war(s), as a demobilization center. The Civilian Conservation Corps (1933-1942) occupied the site between the wars. Part of the base's land area hosts the Fort Dix Federal Correctional Institution, the largest federal prison in the country.[29]

Fort Dix, New Jersey, was a U.S. Army base from where many a soldier shipped overseas during World War II. The layout of this pillow cover, with two large roses flanking both sides of a "Mother" poem, is a design we will see frequently on textiles of this type. The poem says, "To one who bears / the sweetest name / And adds a lustre [sic] / to the same [...]." 16.125" x 17". 1941-1945. $25-35.

Camp Davis, North Carolina, built in December 1940, was used from April 1941 as a training camp for anti-aircraft artillery by the First U.S. Army, 4th Corps. The base area had 3,000 buildings and covered more than 45,000 acres of land. It officially closed in 1946, like so many other bases that were hurriedly set up to meet wartime needs. For a time, the site was used by the U.S. Navy, which apparently returned the leased land to landowners. In 1954, the Marines again leased the land and continue to occupy the site.[30]

In layout of design, this rayon U.S. Army pillow cover from Camp Davis, North Carolina, is similar to the previous pillow cover. The focus of this textile is "Friendship" and it includes this poem: "No road is too long / If at the end / We find a welcome from a friend. / A cheery handclasp / Warm and true / Is always good / From a pal like you." This has two stains on the back. 15.75" x 17.75". 1940-1945. $15-20.

Fort Custer Training Center in Michigan is called Fort Custer, for short. Set up in 1917, the U.S. Army site was named to honor Union General George Armstrong Custer (1839-1876),[31] who fought during the American Civil War and was present when General Robert E. Lee surrendered. Custer also participated in the Indian Wars and was killed at the Battle of the Little Big Horn ("Custer's Last Stand").

Between the wars, Fort Custer hosted the Civilian Conservation Corps, but with the outbreak of World War II, 300,000 soldiers received training there. The 5th Infantry Division was deployed to Iceland and landed in France directly before D-Day. The Division sustained heavy casualties. Fort Custer held German prisoners of war until 1945 (the end of WWII).[32]

This U.S. Army site at Fort Richardson, Alaska, was built between 1940 and 1941 and was named for military explorer, Brigadier General Wilds P. Richardson (1861-1929).[33] He served in Alaska Territory on active duty in three different time periods between 1897 and 1917. Under his leadership, the Richardson Highway was built, a 380-mile road that connects Valdez and Fairbanks, Alaska. Today, Fort Richardson is still very active. Currently, it is "the primary response force for the Pacific Theater."[34]

An unusual feature of this rayon U.S. Army pillow cover from Fort Custer, Michigan, is the presence of a tag on the front, inserted under the fringe. It says, "Another Velvograph Product/ Water Repellent." The bold and graphic designs flocked onto this pillow include the words "In Service For Our Country" on a service flag; the bold words, "U.S. Army," tanks, and an eagle. The predominant colors of red, white, and blue makes me wonder why the color magenta was chosen for the rayon fringe finish. 16.25" x 16.5". 1941-1945. $20-30.

This charming rayon U.S. Army pillow cover is from Fort Richardson, Alaska. The surface designs include a Native American totem pole, an outline of the shore of Alaska, a bear "patch" that represents Alaska's Department of the Army, and a unique "Mother" poem: "Please make my bed / And dust my chair / For soon dear Mother / I'll be there / To tell you that the war is won / Then you'll be proud of me- / Your Son." This textile has good contrast of colors and a variegated rayon fringe that sets off the color designs very well. 17.25" x 17.5". 1941-1945. $15-20.

Camp Sibert was active from 1942 to 1945. Since that time, concern has arisen over the need to remove dangerous chemical warfare material (CWM) that remains. A chemical cleanup company called "Parsons" was selected by the U.S. Army Corps of Engineers, which hired the outfit to locate and remove material that constitutes a threat to life. To read about the work of the Parsons and their progress, please visit their website.[35]

This magenta color pillow cover made of rayon and with yellow flocking represents the Lovell Hospital at Fort Devens, Massachusetts. The hospital is named for General Joseph Lovell (1788-1836), the Army's first surgeon general who served in that capacity for eighteen years, beginning in 1818.

Fort Devens was established as Camp Devens in 1917. The following year, it functioned as a separation center for soldiers returning from Europe (World War I). In 1931, Fort Devens was granted permanent status as a U.S. Army base and in the early years of World War II, base housing greatly increased and Moore Army Airfield was added. In all, more than one million soldiers trained at the site. Fort Devens was discontinued in 1996 as a result of a Congressional Act: "The Base Realignment and Closing Act."[37]

I was happy to collect this rare pillow cover from Camp Sibert, Gadsden, Alabama. During World War II, Camp Sibert was a chemical warfare training camp. This textile, in yellow, red, and blue, features a "Mother" poem, which has appeared on other pillows in this compilation. "To one who bears the sweetest name / and adds a luster to the same [...]." 15.875" x 16.625". 1942-1945. $15-20.

A large eagle motif takes center stage on this rayon U.S. Army cover from Lovell Hospital, Fort Devens, Massachusetts. This pillow cover's condition proves that it has been used, yet because Fort Devens was home to a very important rehabilitation hospital, the pillow cover is of more value than others in similar condition. 16.625" x 17.75". 1941-1945. $10-20.

This pillow cover is proof that various artists hand-painted the designs on pillow covers for Camp Bowie. The "puce" color background of this elegant looking textile is just the right color to set off its beautifully rendered roses. One can just imagine the feeling that someone would have experienced in receiving this message of friendship from "far away."

This Camp Bowie, Texas, pillow cover made of acetate is another example of a hand-painted textile. This one features roses. The painter's signature looks like "Egora" or possibly "E. Gora." The poem is titled "Just Hello!" and reads: "I'd like to be with you awhile / And hear about the folks / I'd like to sit and see you smile / At the same old jokes / But since you are so far away / I cannot hope to go / I'll send along this little token / Just to say "Hello"!" A large eagle motif is at top center. 16" x 16". 1940-1946. $20-25. *Courtesy of Lyell D. Henry.*

Camp Bowie is named for James Bowie (1796-1836), a Texas patriot killed at the Battle of the Alamo. The Camp was one of the largest training centers in Texas during World War II. The first group to train there in 1940 was the 36th Division of the Texas National Guard. During the war, the site served as a detention center for 2,700 German prisoners of war who worked as day laborers on central Texas farms. In 1946, the Camp was discontinued, although it exists in a more limited capacity today.[38]

Hand-painted roses rendered by an artist named "Lund" make a striking statement on this acetate U.S. Army pillow cover from Camp Bowie, Texas. A "Sweetheart" poem says: "Until you and I shall meet again / Sweet thoughts of love to you I send / May all my blessings be with you / Your sweetheart always True." 16" x 17". 1940-1946. $20-25.

Please refer to former entries about Fort Leonard Wood

This acetate U.S. Army pillow cover from Fort Leonard Wood, Missouri, presents four (unnamed) action scenes, plus images of a "Service Club" and a "Field House." The following "Sister" poem is listed, "Someone I love / I know loves me / Sister of mine / true as can be. / Ever I think of the / happy days flown / Remembering you always / Sister my own." A symbol "A 5" appears at the bottom. 15.75" x 17.75". 1940-1945. $20-25. *Courtesy of Lyell D. Henry.*

This acetate U.S. Army pillow cover from Fort Leonard Wood, Missouri, features roses and a "Mother" poem: "To one who bears / the sweetest name, / And adds a luster / to the same. A large symbol is present that represents the 5th Army. […]." The pillow cover is in great shape, except for the creases sustained by being stored, folded in fourths. 16.375" x 17.375". 1940-1945. $25-35. *Courtesy of Lyell D. Henry.*

To read more about Camp McCoy, please see an entry in Chapter Two. One is lucky, indeed, to find pillow covers that are in a pristine condition. This one is not in good condition and the value placed on it reflects that status. Be sure to check out the chapter of this book that will tell you how to store textile items to better preserve them. Nevertheless, this rayon U.S. Army pillow cover features roses and a common, short "Mother" poem: "Never a pal so near, / No comrade half so true, / Never a friend so dear / Mother of mine, as you." 17" x 16.75". 1941-1945. $5-10. *Courtesy of Lyell D. Henry.*

Camp Kilmer, New Jersey, is named for (Alfred) Joyce Kilmer (1886-1918), a World War I soldier who was killed at the Second Battle of the Marne. He is most famous for his poem, "Trees." The 332nd Engineer Service Regiment, trained at Camp Claiborne, Louisiana, was the first unit to arrive at the site on July 22, 1942. During World War II, more than 2-1/2 million soldiers were processed through the camp while in transit to or from the European front. Deactivated in 1949, the Camp reopened in 1955 during the Cold War and officially closed in 2009.[39]

This "Mother" pillow cover has an unusual silver background on which four roses are artistically painted. A red, white, and blue eagle motif is centered above a poem: "Never a pal so near / No comrade half so true. / Never a friend so dear / Mother of mine, as you." This is a souvenir of Camp Ripley, Minnesota, opened in 1930 and was named for the former military site, Fort Ripley, which closed in 1877. However, the pillow cover is difficult to place in time, as the Camp is currently under the jurisdiction of the Minnesota National Guard and its land holdings equal 53,000 acres since an addition in 1971. This textile has a small stain. 16.625" x 16.625". Circa 1950s. $10-15. *Courtesy of Lyell D. Henry.*

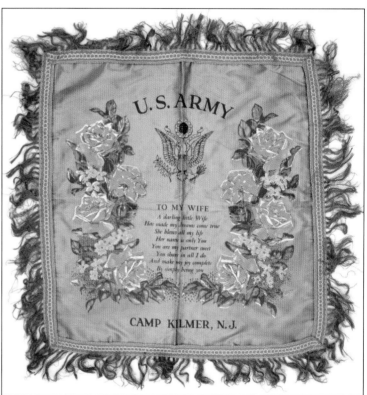

Roses flank both sides of a "To My Wife" poem that is present on this rayon U.S. Army pillow cover from Camp Kilmer, New Jersey. The poem says, "A darling little Wife / Has made my dreams come true / She blesses all my life / Her name is only You / You are a partner sweet / You share in all I do / And make my joy complete / By simply being you." 16.25" x 17". 1942-1949. $15-20. *Courtesy of Lyell D. Henry.*

Antique and used items do not have to be perfect for us to enjoy them. Like a great-grandmother with wrinkles, who still has good advice to give, we must sometimes overlook the flaws and appreciate what can be learned from these historically important textiles, some of which have been around for almost one hundred years! This rayon U.S. Army, yellow-green pillow cover from Camp Hood, Texas, features a unique "Mother" poem: "She's a lot of fun to be with / She's peppy and she's sweet, / She's always understanding / She's a pal who's hard to beat. / And I have loved her very much / Since I was very small, / For my Mom is a darling ~ / And she really tops them all." The delicate images of roses are flocked, and appear to have been hand-painted. The edges of this pillow cover are in severe disrepair, but, with patience, could be reset and re-sewn. This is in used condition. 16.125" x 17.25". 1942-1950. $3-5 (possibly more, if repaired). *Courtesy of Lyell D. Henry.*

Fort Benning, Georgia, as we have previously seen, was formerly called Camp Benning and was initially established during World War I. This particular pillow cover is rendered in three colors of red, blue, and yellow on a white rayon background.

Images of jet planes and soldiers on the ground are printed on this tri-color rayon U.S. Army "Sweetheart" pillow cover from Fort Benning, Georgia. The poem says, "Sweetheart darling / I think of you / Although we're / far apart I see / you always / because you're in / my heart." This textile features retroactive images. 16.75" x 16.5". Circa late 1950s-early 1960s. $5-10. *Courtesy of Lyell D. Henry.*

Previously, Fort Knox was known as Camp Knox (from 1918-1925 and 1928-1931). Between 1925 and 1928, it was simply a national forest. Today, it is the site of the General George S. Patton Museum. Renamed Fort Knox in 1932, most Americans know the site as the repository for most of America's gold bullion resources. The military base offered basic training and served as the headquarters for the U.S. Army Armor School. That unit is scheduled to move to Fort Benning, Georgia, in 2011.[40]

Blue-gray is the background color of this rayon U.S. Army pillow with printed images from Fort Knox, Kentucky. Featured are two large roses on either side of a "To My Wife" poem: "A darling little Wife / Has made my dreams come true / [...]" The burnt orange, cotton fringe is a complementary color to the background. 15.25" x 16.5". 1941-1945. $5-10. *Courtesy of Lyell D. Henry.*

Fort Riley has been in continuous use since 1853 when it was established as a military outpost to assist travelers on the Oregon California and Santa Fe trails, at a time of great migration. The fort was very active during World War II and is still in use today by the 1st Infantry Division. The site is named for Major General Bennett C. Riley (1787-1853), who in 1829 "led the first military escort along the Santa Fe trail."[41]

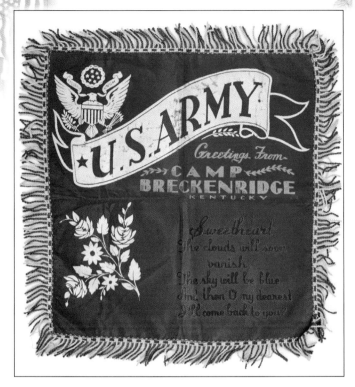

Like most pillow covers of the era, this one has been folded in fourths and kept in a drawer for many years. Textiles like these were probably seen as expendable commodities and no one ever expected that they would be prized so much. All of the motifs and letters are flocked on this U.S. Army rayon pillow cover with "Greetings from Camp Breckenridge, Kentucky." The overall color scheme is red, blue, and yellow, and the cover has a yellow and blue fringe. A "Sweetheart" poem, in indigo blue lettering, says: "The clouds will soon /vanish / The sky will be blue / And then O my dearest / I'll come back to you!" 20" x 20". Circa 1950s. $16-26.

The U.S. Army's 1st Infantry Division at Fort Riley, Kansas, is called to mind by this acetate, "Sweetheart" pillow cover. The following poem is included: "I thought that you / would like to know / That someone's thoughts / go where you go. […]" The only difference in the poem from the last pillow cover we viewed is that more of the letters are capitalized. This is in pristine condition and never used. There are a few fold lines. 16.5" x 17.375". Circa 1941-1945. $30-40 *Courtesy of Lyell D. Henry.*

Certain poems seem to have been favorites and are repeated on many pillows, across the various branches of service, as you shall see. Sometimes, there is a change of only one word, such as "Mother," instead of "Sweetheart," or "Mother" to "Grandmother." The rules of standard punctuation and capitalization are not observed and quite often punctuation is non-existent. In retyping poetry, here, there has been no attempt to simulate the original display of words. This is yet another acetate U.S. Army, printed pillow cover from Fort Dix, New Jersey, with scenes that are repeated on other covers we have seen. The "Sweetheart" poem is the one that begins "I thought that you / would like to know / that someone's thoughts / go where you go. […]." This is missing some of its turquoise fringe and has slight stains on the back. 15.75" x 16.75". 1942-1945. $10-15. *Courtesy of Lyell D. Henry.*

Fort Knox was named for Henry Knox (1750-1806), who served in the Revolutionary War as the Chief of Artillery. He was America's first Secretary of War. In July 1940, the 7th Cavalry became the 1st Armored Division, stationed at Fort Knox, Kentucky. By October of the same year, an Armored Force School and Replacement Center were set up on the base.[42] "The U.S. Army Armor Center consists of agencies, directorates, and units that oversee and support operations for the organizations and their missions, which includes The Armor School. The Armor School is responsible for training the current mounted force as well as developing the tools for the future mounted force."[43]

The original manufacturer's paper tag is glued to the backing fabric, which makes this pillow cover more valuable! It says: "SEEMOR PRODUCTS sell more. Seymour Wallas and Company, St. Louis, Missouri." This acetate, U.S. Army pillow cover from Camp Blanding, Florida, features "The Stars and Stripes Forever" and a large image of the United States flag with forty-eight stars. A Jeep carrying soldiers, and an eagle are the two other flocked decorations along with a poem titled "Remembrance:" "I'm glad of the memories / of days you were near, / Each memory I treasure / Each thought I hold dear, / I remember each hour / I remember each day, / You're always beside me / You're with me to stay." The fringe is light red and yellow. 15.5" x 17.5". 1941-1945. $35-40. *Courtesy of Lyell D. Henry.*

This acetate, never used U.S. Army, "Mother" pillow cover from Fort Knox, Kentucky, has the designation "The Armor Center." A large insignia and roses grace an ivory background and the poem, enclosed within a yellow border, says, "To one who bears the sweetest name, / And adds a luster to the same. [...]." 16.5" x 17". Circa 1940-1945. $20-30. *Courtesy of Lyell D. Henry.*

Pink is the overwhelming color choice of this generic U.S. Army acetate pillow cover that has been printed with scenes of soldiers wearing hats that indicate a provenance of "between the wars" or "early World War II." The featured poem is the same "Sweetheart" one we will see many times, "I thought that you would like to know / That someone's thoughts go where you go. [...]" A distinctive fringe in variegated threads sets off the coloration of the eagle, which is straddling an American flag. This item shows some fold marks, but has never been used. 15.875" x 16.125". 1918-1942. $40-50. *Courtesy of Lyell D. Henry.*

Camp Tyson, Tennessee, was the country's only barrage balloon training center during World War II. The balloons, used in coastal defense, by air, were filled with helium or hydrogen and the exterior was a combination of a two-ply cotton fabric "impregnated with synthetic rubber."[44] Camp Tyson was the site where soldiers were taught to build, fly, and maintain these defense balloons that measured thirty-five feet across and eighty-five feet long.

Named for Brigadier General Lawrence D. Tyson, a World War I veteran, Camp Tyson went into construction in 1941. By the end of World War II, it is estimated that the military site held 20,000 soldiers or more. The base was deactivated after the war, and the property was acquired by the H. C. Spinks Clay Company, according to Robert Parkinson, University of Tennessee, Knoxville.[45]

Camp Mackall is a U.S. Army base whose name honors Private John Thomas Mackall (1920-1942) of Wellsville, Ohio. A member of the 2nd Battalion, 503rd Parachute Infantry Regiment, "Tommy" Mackall participated in Operation Torch as part of the Allied invasion of North Africa during World War II. Seven paratroopers were instantly killed when a French Vichy aircraft attacked their plane as it landed. Mackall was injured and died on November 12, 1942. Camp Mackall remains an active military facility today where training exercises are conducted for members of the U.S. Army Special Forces. In particular, they are versed in techniques to use if captured by the enemy. The military base was renamed Camp Mackall in 1943.[46]

Camp Mackall, North Carolina, is the military base where this acetate pillow cover, in red, white, and blue, originated. The images depicted, in flocking, are planes, paratroops, and an eagle within a circle. The Latin words, *Vincit qui primum gerit*," under the eagle, mean "He conquers who gets there first." This textile is wrinkled, but to try to "improve" it would be to destroy it. Application of steam and/or dry cleaning will remove flocking. Paratroop items are very much in demand. 16.125" x 16.375". 1942-1945. $25-40. *Courtesy of Lyell D. Henry.*

An odd combination of colors is employed in this rayon U.S. Army pillow cover from Camp Tyson, Tennessee. A large purple eagle carries a yellow banner with the Latin words "e pluribus unum." A circle under the eagle's left wing has an image and the words "Barrage Balloon." Two red roses were hand painted by "Ness." A poem says, "When the golden / sun is sinking, / And your mind from / troubles free, / While of others you / are thinking, / Will you sometimes / think of me?" 16.125" x 16.625". 1941-1945. $17-30.

Please refer to the previously provided background information about Camp Blanding

A light gray fabric that looks like crepe is used as the background for large roses and other flocked designs on this Camp Blanding, Florida, pillow cover. This fabric is quite unusual and is the first of its kind seen for use in making a World War II item of this type. A "Mother and Dad" poem says, "No one knows but mother and Dad / about the smiles and tears we've had / No one is willing and glad to share / whatever we have of joy or care / no others of years gone by / or understand each smile and sigh / for the dearest hearts / on this old earth / are the hearts at home / of golden worth." The surface has nice flocking that is highly textured, in red and lime green colors. A yellow fringe is present. This pillow cover appears to have mold growing on its surface, and the light blue backing also shows signs of mold. 15.5" x 18.75". 1940-1945. This item has no resale value. *Courtesy of Lyell D. Henry.*

Generic pillow covers such as this one were very handy because they could be sold at any U.S. Army installation. The poem on this pillow cover sums up the thoughts of many who go to war: a wish to be remembered, now, and perhaps, later. This printed design is complex and artistically rendered, with a large eagle straddling an American flag (as we have seen before). Above a battle scene is the poem, "Remember Me": "It is sweet to be remembered / When you're feeling sad and blue / It sets the pulse to throbbing / And it cheers the heart up too / It makes the world worth living / to be remembered just by you." Looking at the helmets, James Cummings, a former soldier of the U.S. Army, judges this textile to be a "between the wars" pillow cover. 16.125" x 15.875". 1918-1942. $25-30. *Courtesy of Lyell D. Henry.*

This generic U.S. Army pillow cover for "Sweetheart" shows a woman in a green dress with a white, ruffled collar, sitting at a table reading a letter. The poem says, "I would like you to know, / my thoughts are where / you go, that I never can / forget our happiness, / since first we met." This is a bit of a variation on a similar poem we have seen. A small stain, the size of a pea, is located on the back and there is a tiny amount of surface damage to the main motif. 17.5" x 18.25". 1941-1945. $10-20.

Fort Bliss, Texas, a place for training anti-aircraft artillery battalions during World War II, has been in continuous use by the U.S. Army since 1849. Occupying a land area of 1,700 square miles, the base is located in New Mexico and Texas, and is the second largest Army installation.[47] It is named in honor of William Wallace Smith Bliss (1815-1853), an Army officer who distinguished himself by his fluency in thirteen foreign languages. He fought in the Mexican American War.[48]

Camp Shelby, Kentucky, was named to honor Isaac Shelby (1750-1826), Indian fighter, Revolutionary War hero, and the first (and fifth) governor of Kentucky.[49] The Camp opened in 1917 and trained members of many branches of military service during World War II. It was home to the Japanese-American 442nd Regiment Combat Team, the 100th Battalion, and the Women's Army Corps (WAC). A prisoner of war camp on the site held members of the German Afrika Corps. After World War II, Camp Shelby was shut down for a period of time, but reopened during the Korean Conflict.[50]

This rayon U.S. Army pillow cover from Fort Bliss, Texas, carries a "To My Wife" poem that is a variation of a similar one we have seen before. "A lovely, darling, little wife / Has made my dreams come true / She's lightened all the cares of life / Her name my sweet, is "You." / My memories are quite complete / You share in all I do. / My heart's a sanctum that I keep / Reserved for thoughts of YOU." All of the motifs are flocked (raised) and include a tank, a Jeep, armaments, a lone soldier on foot, a plane, and an eagle. The poem is in red, and the fringe has rose and yellow strands. This pillow cover has sustained damage due to use. 16.5" x 17.75". 1941-1945. $5-10. *Courtesy of Lyell D. Henry.*

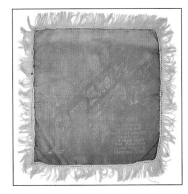

This acetate U.S. Army "Sweetheart" pillow cover from Camp Shelby, Mississippi, employs low loft flocking in yellow for all of its words and designs. The poem reads: "Love unending / Warm and true / Sweetheart mine this / brings to you [...]." There is major color loss along the top edge of this textile, perhaps due to exposure to ultraviolet rays if it was draped over the top of a couch near a sunny window. 16.25" x 16.875". 1941-1945. $3-5.

Camp Pickett, Virginia, is named for Confederate General George Pickett (1825-1875). A former Civilian Conservation Corps camp, it was converted to an Army base in 1941, when the threat of war became more imminent. Two railways and Blackstone Army Airfield were added, the latter being large enough to land Douglas C-47 planes, sometimes called "Gooney Birds." The base was virtually unchanged from the 1940s to the 1990s. In 1997, the site was officially turned over to the Virginia National Guard.[51]

The Kelly Green color of this rayon U.S. Army pillow cover from Camp Pickett, Virginia is very attractive. It is only on closer inspection that one sees that the edges of the pillow top have become totally unattached from the edge treatment (fringe) and are hanging in shreds. This textile is smaller than usual. It features a "Just Hello" poem that says, " I'd like to be with you / and hear about the folks / I'd like to see you smile / at the same old jokes / But since you are so far away / I cannot hope to go / I'll send this little token / Just to say HELLO!" Decorations in yellow flocking include a "V" for Victory symbol and an eagle. 12" x 12". 1941-1945. $3-5.

Japan surrendered unconditionally on August 15, 1945, a day that is now known as "V-J Day" ("Victory over Japan"). On September 2, 1945, Japanese officials boarded the *U.S.S. Missouri*, moored at Pearl Harbor, to sign a peace treaty. From that day until April 28, 1952, Japan was under occupation by Allied Forces, led by the United States, and supported by Australia, India, New Zealand, and the United Kingdom.[52]

Located at the confluence of the Mississippi and Minnesota rivers, this military site was first called Fort Anthony. The base underwent further construction between 1820 and 1824 by the 5th Regiment, U.S. Army Infantry, and when the work was finished, it was renamed Fort Snelling, in honor of Colonel Josiah Snelling (1782-1828), the commander of that unit.[53]

During World War II, soldiers were provided Japanese language instruction at the site's Military Intelligence Service Language School. On October 12, 1946, Fort Snelling was deactivated. Today, the land area serves as a National Historic Landmark and a park, managed by various operatives, including the National Park Service.[54]

This acetate pillow cover with a map of Okinawa was sold as having come from "Occupied Japan," but may have a later date of origin, if the jet on its surface is any indication. A sailboat, a battleship, a man balancing two buckets on his shoulders, and a plane are the scenes depicted on this textile, with its predominantly pink and turquoise coloration on a white background. In addition, the location of the "Ernie Pyle Memorial" is noted on the island of Ie Shima. The memorial to Ernie Pyle (1900-1945) is one of only three such tributes that were allowed to remain on Okinawa after the Japanese resumed jurisdiction of the island. Pyle, a Pulitzer winning news correspondent for the Scripps Howard Company, was shot by Japanese sniper fire and died in 1945 at Ie Shima. This pillow cover is in mint condition. 17.25" x 18.25". This textile obviously dates to a time after Pyle's death, later than 1945. $20-30.

This U.S. Army "Sweetheart" pillow cover is from Fort Snelling, Minnesota. The printed rayon textile features the following named scenes: 1) "Field Artillery," 2) "Scout Car," 3) "Infantry with Garand Rifle," 4) "Old Round Tower," 5) "Antiaircraft Gun," 6) "Flying Fortress," and 7) "Tank." The poem states, "Until you and I shall meet again / Sweet thoughts of love to you I send / And though I am so far away / Remembering you day-by-day / May all my blessings be with you / Your sweetheart always true." The poem is copyrighted by the "B.B. Company." This item was never used. 16" x 16.375". 1941-1946. $20-25.

This spun rayon pillow cover with a black background was made in Japan and carries a "Sweetheart" poem: "I love you when you're laughing, / I love you when you're sad, / I love you when you're teasing, / I love you when you're glad, / I love you when you're fooling, / I love you when you're true, / And the reason why I love you, / Is just because you're you." The poem is enclosed within a heart. Roses and lovebirds complete the design. The backing (of unknown material) is red. There is an unusually short, 1" fringe. 12" x 12". 1945-1952. $10-16.

This "Stars and Stripes Forever" acetate pillow cover features a large, American flag with forty-eight stars. Its "Sweetheart" poem says, "I thought that you / would like to know / That someone's thought / go where you go […]." There are planes in the sky, in formation, on the left side, and additional planes on the right. On the ground are soldiers and equipment, charging into battle. This has a raspberry color fringe. This textile is in mint condition. 15.875" x 16.25". 1941-1945. $25-35.

Camp Ashland, Nebraska, an 878-acre site, was intended to be just a temporary camp when it was set up with tents during World War II for use by the Nebraska National Guard.[55] Today, the site has been updated and serves as home to the Army National Guard and the U.S. Army Reserve.[56]

When Camp Claiborne was established in 1930, it was named Camp Evangeline. The 23,000-acre site was renamed for William Charles Cole Claiborne (1772-1817),[57] Louisiana's first governor from 1812 to 1816. During World War II, more than a million soldiers received basic training and artillery practice here. Toward the end of the war, the site was home to German prisoners of war. Deactivated in 1945, the land is now managed by the National Park Service.[58]

Dusty yellow is the background color of this unusual acetate U.S. Army pillow cover from Camp Ashland, Nebraska. The printed poem for "Mother" can be seen in large fancy letters. The words say, "Each petal represents a flower, / Each bud a kiss for you, / Each stem an arm entwined about / My Mother, dear and true." A large U.S. Army insignia has been printed at top center, and a "U" shape spray of roses and rose buds, printed in black, appear under the poem. 15.125" x 16.375". 1941-1945. $10-20. *Courtesy of Lyell D. Henry.*

Large, stylized letters form the word "Remembrance" at the top of this rayon U.S. Army pillow cover that features a "V" for "Victory." This acetate item is from Camp Claiborne, Louisiana, and presents a poem by the same name, "Remembrance." It says, "It is nice to remember / With wishes for cheer / Someone like you / Growing dearer / each year. / It's nice to remember / Someone like you. / but it's sweet to know / You're remembering, too." This item has the expected and usual fold lines, but was never used. It has a gray-green fringe. 16.375" x 17.125". 1941-1945. $20-30. *Courtesy of Lyell D. Henry.*

Red flocked motifs, including an eagle, flags, and a laurel wreath, as well as words, are present on this rayon U.S. Army pillow cover from San Antonio, Texas. Its "Mother" poem is rendered in blue flocking. It says, "There's a certain lovely Mother / who is loyal, sweet and true - / One whose love and understanding / Does what nothing else could do / In providing smiles and comfort - / Everything in life that's fine - / She's a darling, and I love her - / And I'm mighty glad she's MINE!" The fringe is yellow and gray. The lower part of the backing is slightly ripped, perhaps due to pillow removal. 15.25" x 16.375". 1941-1945. $5-10. *Courtesy of Lyell D. Henry.*

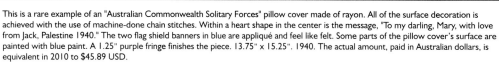

This is a rare example of an "Australian Commonwealth Solitary Forces" pillow cover made of rayon. All of the surface decoration is achieved with the use of machine-done chain stitches. Within a heart shape in the center is the message, "To my darling, Mary, with love from Jack, Palestine 1940." The two flag shield banners in blue are appliqué and feel like felt. Some parts of the pillow cover's surface are painted with blue paint. A 1.25" purple fringe finishes the piece. 13.75" x 15.25". 1940. The actual amount, paid in Australian dollars, is equivalent in 2010 to $45.89 USD.

Fort Winfield Scott, California, was first established in the 1850s on the site of the old Spanish "Castillo de San Joaquín," that is, "Castle of Saint Joaquín." By U.S. Army Order #133, in 1882 it was named after General Winfield Scott (1786-1866). "Old Fuss and Feathers," a 47-year career Army man, was a hero of the Mexican War. In 1838 and 1839, his order from President Martin Van Buren was to remove Native American Cherokees from Cherokee Nation in Georgia and relocate them in Oklahoma. Thousands of Indians, mostly forced to march on foot, succumbed to disease and death, especially the very young and the elderly, on what is now known as the "Trail of Tears."[59]

Scott was a strategist in the Civil War, on the Union side, famous for masterminding the Anaconda Plan that helped to win the war against the Confederacy. In addition, Scott was his Whig Party's nominee for president over incumbent Millard Fillmore, but lost to Franklin Pierce of New Hampshire, our 14th president, who served in office from 1853-1857.

Just four years after being named "Fort Winfield Scott," the site was reclassified as a sub-post of the Presidio of San Francisco. It was not until 1912 that use of the post's former name was resumed. Fort Winfield Scott served as the overseer of coastal security in the area, although its boundaries of jurisdiction seem never to have been clearly defined. To enter the site, one has to pass under a bridge that is marked, "Fort Winfield Scott," a name that is inscribed on a cement overpass. On June 1, 1946, the Army's Coastal Artillery School was transferred to Fort Monroe, Virginia. The base, as an independent unit, appears to have ended on June 25, 1946. In 1981, the 504th Military Police Battalion used the facilities.[60]

This "Remembrance" pillow cover is rare indeed. The blue lettering and motifs are set on a red background of undetermined fibers. A printed poem titled "Remembering" says: "It's nice to remember / With wishes for cheer, / Someone like you / growing dearer each year. / It's nice to remember / Someone like you -- / But it's sweeter to know / You're remembering too." 14.625" x 16.5". 1924-1946. $35-50. *Courtesy of Lyell D. Henry.*

The U.S. Army site referred to in "Indio, California" was actually an 18,000-square-mile location that included area in California, Arizona, and Nevada. The desert land area was selected by General George Patton for training soldiers in desert warfare in preparation for the invasion of North Africa in November 1942. Patton's 1st Armored Corps was trained at CAMA, as it was called, followed by the 2nd Armored Corps, and the 4th, 9th, 15th, and 10th Army Corps. After the Allied victory in North Africa, there was no more need for desert warfare training and the base closed in 1944.[61]

This silk U.S. Army pillow cover features a large eagle and flag on a beige background. By now, we have seen the sole word "Mother" numerous times, especially on World War I pillow covers. This textile offers the word, design, "Father," and a location, "Indio, California." The training base in the area of Indio was open from 1942-1944. Unfortunately, this rare example is very soiled and is torn in a linear fashion horizontally. It has a .75" fringe. This is wonderful for the history lesson it elicits, but is in poor condition. 15.875" x 17.375". $5-10. *Courtesy of Lyell D. Henry.*

The same "Mother" poem appears on these rayon U.S. Army pillow covers: "To one who bears / the sweetest name / And adds a luster / to the same [...]." On the first, two large pink roses flank each side of the poem. The fringe is also pink. The backing is torn and seems to be ripped along the previous sewing line that closed up the bottom. 15.375" x 16". 1941-1945. $10-20. The second is from Fort Benning, Georgia. In this case, the roses are painted on and the "registration marks" do not quite line up. It is in mint condition, but with four fold lines visible. 17" x 17.25". 1941-1945. $25-35. *Courtesy of Lyell D. Henry.*

Camp Ripley, just north of Little Falls, Minnesota, was a National Guard site. In February 1941, the Minnesota National Guard became part of the 34th Infantry Division. After the war, the Camp returned to the jurisdiction of the National Guard.[62]

This acetate U.S. Army pillow cover's top has separated from the fringe on the left side. Its yellow fringe is matted. However, this textile is important because of its distinctive "Mother" poem and its striking colors and designs. All of the surface decorations are flocked. The poem says, "I always think of mother / no matter where I roam. / I always think of mother / although I'm far from home. / Friends and many others / sometimes prove untrue, / but never does a mother / for her heart is always true." An emblem of the U.S. Army, with an eagle and the initials, "U.S.A.," are prominent on this item, as well as the word "Mother." This is in used condition. 16.125" x 16.125". Circa 1950s. $5-10.

This acetate U.S. Army pillow cover from Camp Ripley, Minnesota, has four painted roses and rose buds that surround a "Mother" poem. The poem says, "Never a pal so near, / No comrade half so true, / Never a friend so dear / Mother of mine, as you." This item was previously used and is slightly stained on the left front and ripped at the bottom where it was once sewn tight to enclose a pillow. The fringe and background are gray, and the U.S. Army emblem is located at center top. 16.75" x 16.75". 1941-1945. $5-10. *Courtesy of Lyell D. Henry.*

Camp Roberts, California, is named for Corporal Harold W. Roberts (1895-1918), who lost his life by drowning during World War I. He accidentally drove a tank into a tank trap that was filled with ten feet of water. He courageously pushed his comrade to safety, knowing that only one of them could get out alive. Posthumously, he was awarded the Medal of Honor. The incident happened when he was in the Montrebeau Forest in northeastern France, a part of the St. Mihel and Meuse-Argonne Offensives.

He was under heavy artillery fire by the Germans. He was only twenty-two years old when he died, had just been promoted to Corporal, and was a member of Company A, 344th Light Tank Battalion. He is buried in France.[63]

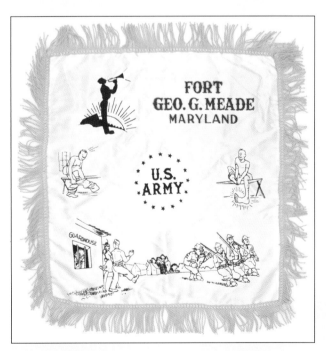

Here we have a comical look at the dangers of enlisting in the U.S. Army, from sore, burning feet, to a drill sergeant keeping you in line, to being stuck in the "Guardhouse" as a happy couple saunters by, and finally, to a man pulling on trousers that appear to be too large. This acetate pillow cover has red letters for the name of the base, "Fort George G. Meade, Maryland," and the rest of the motifs are flocked in blue. This item is in mint condition. 16.125" x 17.125". 1941-1945. $35-45.

Camp Roberts is only one of two bases ever named for an enlisted man, and the only base of that kind that still exists. The land area (42,784 acres) of Camp Roberts once was inhabited by Native Americans and Spanish explorers, according to Master Sergeant Al Davis (Retired, US Army) in his online essay, "Historic California Posts: Camp Roberts."[64] A Replacement Training Center opened in 1941 and during World War II, approximately 436,000 soldiers trained there. The Camp was closed by the U.S. Army in 1970, but re-opened in 1971 for use by the Reserve Component Training Center of the California Army National Guard.[64]

One could almost miss the words "Camp Roberts, California," that are almost hidden on this rayon U.S. Army pillow cover by a serged ruffle. This "Mother'" pillow has the following beautiful words, "God took the sunshine / from the skies, / And made the love light in your eyes, / From honeyed flowers He took the dew / And made your tears unselfish, true / Upon a rock your faith he built, / With angel prayers your breath / He filled, / And with His love made yours divine, / But best of all He made you mine." The background is turquoise and the stylized graphics include two bluebirds, a cottage with a path, and some roses, all printed motifs. This is in mint condition, with the exception of some residue from a piece of masking tape (price label) on the backing. 16.125" x 16.125". 1941-1945. $35-55. *Courtesy of Lyell D. Henry.*

According to a "wiki" file, this military location was named for President Andrew Jackson, a former U.S. Army general.[65] He served in the office of president from 1829-1837. When the site was built in 1917, it was called "Camp Jackson." Between the wars, it was abandoned, but it was reactivated as a basic combat training camp for the U.S. Army during World War II. Richard E. Osborne's book, *World War II Sites in the United States*, states that Fort Jackson trained more than one-half million troops during that war, including the 8th, 77th, and 30th Infantry divisions. Today, this is still an active military base. The history of the site is preserved in the Fort Jackson Museum.[66]

A rayon U.S. Army pillow cover, from Fort Jackson, South Carolina, features a color combination of red, yellow, and blue on a white background. A unique "Mother" poem says, "A MOTHER dear and sweet as you / Is such a rare delight / Because your loving thoughtful ways / Make life more fine and bright / You share when I am sad or glad / The DEAREST one I ever had." This was never used. The images of jets indicate a provenance date that is later than World War II. 18.375" x 19.125". Post 1945. $15-20.

Yellow is the background color of this miniature, rayon pillow cover from the U.S. Army. Featured is a "Mother and Dad" poem: "No one knows but Mother and Dad / About the smiles and tears we've had […]." All designs are printed and the predominantly blue color fringe is about .5" long. The backing is a black and turquoise textured fabric of large abstract flowers. The bottom edge is finished poorly, in an uneven manner, but the piece appears to have never been used. Its diminutive size makes this a rare item. 10.25" x 10.75". 1941-1945. $30-35. *Courtesy of Lyell D. Henry.*

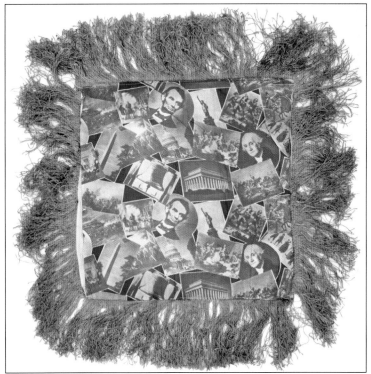

This rayon pillow cover looks deceptively familiar, as it resembles others in this collection, but it is very unique. The 5.5" brown fringe is the longest we have seen on any pillow, even those of the World War I era. The "Mother" poem says, "M is for the million things she gave me / O means only that she's growing old […]." This pillow cover is rare and never used. 15.75" x 16". Circa 1942-1943. $45-55. *Courtesy of Lyell D. Henry.*

This is the beautiful backing fabric of the last pillow cover. Featuring images of Abraham Lincoln and George Washington, the 100 percent cotton fabric, in blue monochromatic hues, presents many scenes around the capitol. One tourist attraction is the Washington Monument, built between 1848 and 1884. It stands at 555' and 5 1/8".

Camp Barkeley's name is actually misspelled. It should have been Camp "Barkley." The Camp was named for David Bennes Barkley (1899-1918). As a young soldier, he died of leg cramps after successfully swimming across the Meuse River in France to find out the exact location of the Germans. He was given a Medal of Honor, posthumously.

This rayon U.S. Army pillow cover from Camp Barkeley, Texas, is easy to date. Built in 1940, the Camp was completed in 1942 and disbanded in 1945. The images are named (clockwise): 1) "Field Artillery," 2) "Scout Car," 3) "Infantryman with Garand Rifle," 4) "Anti-aircraft Gun," 5) "Flying Fortress," and 6) "Tank." The poem, "To My Sister," says, "Nice to chat with / good to know /Glad to have her / where I go. / Kind in trouble / bright in joy, / Suits exactly – can't say why / Sweet and wholesome, / always true / That's my sister, / yes, that's you." This item has been used and was torn along tight machine stitching lines that once held in a pillow form. 16.125" x 16.5". 1942-1945. $5-10. *Courtesy of Lyell D. Henry.*

Camp Barkeley hosted the 45th Infantry Division and the 11th and 12th Armored Divisions and trained pilots at its Abilene Air Field during World War II. The Air Field was renamed Dyess Air Force Base in 1956. German prisoners of war were kept at the Camp and numbered 840 by 1945.[67]

Camp Howze in Gainesville, Texas, was built in 1941 and was first occupied by the U.S. Army 1942 as a much-needed infantry replacement training center. The site was named in remembrance of Major Robert Lee Howze (1864-1926), who crossed a frozen river with the 6th Cavalry to engage the Brulé Sioux Indians, a sub-tribe of Lakota Sioux American Indians. For his efforts, he won the Medal of Honor.

During World War II, Camp Howze could house close to 40,000 troops and was "home" to the 84th, 86th, and 103rd Divisions. German prisoners of war stayed at the Camp during World War II. No longer needed after the war, the camp closed in 1946.

Someone apparently folded this exquisite rayon U.S. Army pillow cover from Camp Howze, Texas, and kept it in a safe place for many years. The flocking is in an ochre color and the name of the Army base is in red flocking. 16.125" x 16.5". 1941-1946. $30-35.

The unusual feature of this rayon pillow cover is that all the motifs are placed diagonally, including the large letters "U.S.A," an U.S. Army insignia with an eagle, flower sprays, a "Mother" poem, and the name, "Camp Blanding, Florida." The short poem says, "With spirit calm as the summer sear / Moving in sweet serenity […]." The flocking is a deep ochre color and the background was originally a deep blue that has now faded to a blue-violet color. The color of the fringe matches the main designs. This is very clean and never used. 16.5" x 16.375". 1940-1945. $10-20.

Camp Rucker, Alabama, is the designated origin of this pillow cover. Work to construct Fort Rucker began on January 15, 1942. On May 1, 1942, the announcement was made that the camp would be named after Confederate General Edmund Rucker, who died in 1878, giving his life to save another soldier. The base was used from 1942 to 1946 and was occupied by these divisions: the 81st Infantry ("Wildcats"), the 35th Infantry ("Santa Fe"), the 98th Infantry ("Iroquois") and the 66th Infantry. Members of the 66th Infantry Division lost their lives while crossing the English Channel on a troop ship called the *Leopoldville* when it was torpedoed by a German submarine. A total of 1,700 prisoners of war were held at this location. Today, the former base displays a large collection of helicopters in their military museum.[69]

Camp Shelby, Mississippi, is the largest state-owned training site in the country. Acquired by the state of Mississippi in 1934, it was used for a training site for the National Guard. During World War II, the Japanese-American 442nd Regimental Combat team, the 100th Battalion, and members of the Women's Army Corps, all trained there. In addition, members of the German Afrika Corps were detained at the site as prisoners of war.[70]

The flocked, bold graphics, in red and white on a blue background, include a large shield and the words "69th Division, Camp Shelby, Mississippi." The fringe is a white gray. The flocking has a couple of slight breaks. This textile appears has never been used. 16" x 16.5". 1942-1946. $25-30.

On this rayon U.S. Army pillow from Camp Rucker, Alabama, an unusual poem appears in flocking. Titled "To my Mother," it says, "You gave the best years / of your life with joy for me / and robbed yourself with / loving heart – unstintingly / your gentle arms my cradle / once, are weary now / and time has set the seal / of care upon your brow / my MOTHER." A large "V" for "Victory," the words "In service for my country and you," an eagle, the name of the base, and the words "United States Army" are all flocked on a medium blue background. The fringe is yellow and in poor condition. 16.75" x 17.5". Circa 1940s. $6-10.

A very unique "Mother" poem appears on an acetate U.S. Army pillow cover that has weathered a few battles itself. The words on the item from Camp McCoy, Wisconsin, are: "There's just one thought within me / The thought dear Mother of you / And until we meet again / My thought of love to you I send / Though you may be far away / I think of you each hour each day / Through the years my prayers shall be / That God will keep you safe for me." This pillow cover features a U.S. Army insignia and roses that look hand-painted. The background is a light grey and the fringe is a medium gray (and very tattered). The cover is also stained and was previously sewn shut. 15.875" x 17.375". 1943. $3-5, more, if repaired. *Courtesy of Lyell D. Henry.*

Yellow and blue are the exclusive colors used in making this U.S. Army acetate pillow cover from Camp Grant, Illinois. An eagle, completely made by flocking, as are all the other motifs on the pillow top, carries *the e pluribus unum* banner that we see so often on these textiles. The fringe consists of blue and yellow, twisted ply, heavy thread. The poem for "Mother and Dad" says, "In all the years I've known you both / You've planned and strived for me. / Through sacrifice of everything / That could a pleasure be. / This token of love I'm sending to you. / Just as a thought from me." 15" x 16.25". 1941-1945. $10-15.

This rayon "Sister" pillow cover with U.S. Army insignia features the following poem: "Of all the girls I ever knew / There never was one Like you / You're the dearest Pal I ever / knew." The poem and other decorations are flocked. This has a dark yellow and pink fringe. This item has been used. 16.625" x 17.375". 1941-1945. $5-10. *Courtesy of Lyell D. Henry.*

According to an Internet article posted by John Soennichsen, historian of the Angel Island Association, the U.S. Army first set up a post on Angel Island during the American Civil War. In 1900, the site's name was inexplicably changed from "Camp Reynolds" to "Fort McDowell." General Irvin McDowell (1818-1885) led Union troops into battle and later was appointed as Commander of the Department of the Pacific.

Fort McDowell is located near San Francisco in a spot that is favorable as a strategic point of coastal defense. During World War II more than 300,000 troops were processed through the fort before shipping out to the Pacific Theater of operations. Fort McDowell served as a transitional site for prisoners of war who were held there before being more permanently relocated.

Like so many other military sites during World War II, Fort McDowell was declared "surplus" in 1946, although the Army did return there to set up Anti-Aircraft Artillery for a time in the 1950s. In 1963, the entire island was declared a California state park and today is a recreational area that provides opportunities for camping, kayaking, and bicycling. The island is accessible by ferry. For more information, please visit www.angelislandferry.com.

The color orange is present on this rayon "Mother" pillow cover from Fort McDowell, Angel Island, California. The poem says, "M is for the million things she gave me / O means only that she's growing old [...]." Orange is the color chosen for highlighting the hand-painted roses, and it is repeated in the lettering of "San Francisco, California," and in a spray of orange poppies at bottom center. A scenic overview of the area includes: 1) "Alameda," 2) "Presidio," 3) "Fort Winfield Scott," 4) "Golden Gate Bridge," 5) "Marin County," 6) "Fort Baker," 7) "Angel Island/Fort McDowell," 8) "Alcatraz Island," 9) "Golden Gate International Exposition," 10) "Fort Mason," 11) "San Francisco Bridge," 12) "Oakland," 13) "Verba Buena Island," and "Berkeley." The background of the pillow is yellow and the fringe is an ochre color. This bottom edge of the cover is much damaged. 15.625" x 16.875". 1941-1945. $5-10. *Courtesy of Lyell D. Henry.*

This predominantly yellow, rayon pillow cover with a bright yellow fringe is marked "U.S. Army." It features a "Mother" poem: "There's a dear little house inviting, / In a dear little place I know. […]." This looks like an early World War II textile, to judge by the type of helmets the soldiers are wearing. There is no particular base of origin associated with this particular pillow cover. The omnipresent eagle holds a banner with "*e pluribus unum*." Flags and roses are the other design elements. 15.5" x 16.875". Circa late 1930s-early 1940s. Never used. $10-15. *Courtesy of Lyell D. Henry.*

Large, red, flocked letters recall Camp Livingston, Louisiana, on this rayon, U.S. Army pillow cover. All of the words and images are flocked in green, red, or blue. A "Mother and Dad" poem says, "No one knows but Mother and Dad / About the smiles and tears we've had / No other is willing and glad to share / Whatever we have of joy or care. / No others of years gone by. / Or understands each smile and sigh, / For the dearest hearts on this old earth / Are the hearts at home of golden worth." This pillow cover was damaged when a pillow form was removed. 16.25" x 15.75". Circa late 1930s-early 1940s. $5-10. *Courtesy of Lyell D. Henry.*

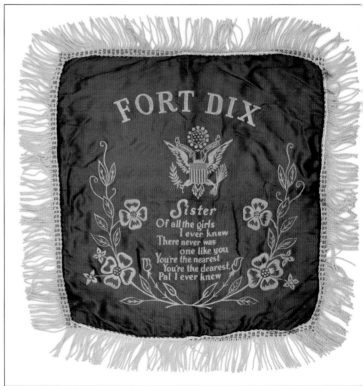

A purple-brown rayon pillow cover with ochre flocking and ochre fringe hails from Fort Dix, Kentucky. Created as a gift for "Sister," this textile has a poem, "Of all the girls / I ever knew / There never was / one like you […]." 16.375" x 16.625". 1941-1945. $10-20. *Courtesy of Lyell D. Henry.*

This special acetate U.S. Army pillow cover presents large images of the Statue of Liberty and a flag, as well as an eagle, and a large banner presents a "Mother" poem: "With spirit calm as the summer sea / Moving in sweet serenity [...]." The background is turquoise; the design elements are mostly white, except for the red lettering of the poem; and the fringe is variegated in yellow and pink. Uncertainty surrounds how the images and poem were applied. The date "1942" appears with "M'c" in the lower left corner. This was never used. 15" x 16". $20-30. *Courtesy of Lyell D. Henry.*

Lots of words appear on this rayon U.S. Army pillow cover from Fort George G. Meade, Maryland, including "Remembrance," "In Service For My Country And You," and a "To my Wife" poem. The words of the poem say, "A darling little wife / has made my dreams come true / she blesses all my life / her name is only you [...]." The background of this acetate pillow is a medium blue and it has a bright yellow fringe. The low-loft, flocked images are in light gray with the flowers over-painted with red paint. The backing fabric has a few stains. 15.25" x 17". 1941-1945. $5-10. *Courtesy of Lyell D. Henry.*

A poem for "Mother" that we now have seen many times is present on this rayon U.S. Army pillow cover from Camp Livingston, Louisiana: "M is for the many things she gave me / O means only that she's growing old [...]." For a change of pace, the banner carried by an eagle says, "Defenders of Our Liberty." The named scenes featured are: 1) "Machine Gun," 2) "Tank," 3) "Anti-Aircraft Gun," 4) "Infantry on Parade," 5) "Long Range Gun," 6) "Field Artillery," and 7) "Anti-Tank Gun." Damage is present due to pillow removal. 15.625" x 17.375". Circa 1930s-1940s. $5-10. *Courtesy of Lyell D. Henry.*

An eagle head, within a shield, is apparently the symbol chosen by the 101st Military Police Company that was in place at Camp Breckenridge, Kentucky, from July 6, 1948 to May 27, 1949. Four unnamed scenes on this rayon pillow cover include: 1) soldiers drilling, 2) soldiers standing at attention, 3) a soldier on patrol, and 4) an American flag keeping watch over the encampment. Pastel turquoise and light pink highlights are superimposed on a pale pink background. The predominant design element is a large eagle and flags at the top of the pillow cover. Roses are present on either side of the cover. Blue felt was used for a backing and is in great condition, with the exception of an ancient piece of masking tape price tag that is clinging for dear life and says $3.00. A smudge of black ink appears on the front of this item that has never been used. 15.875" x 16.125". Circa 1948-1949. $10-20. *Courtesy of Lyell D. Henry.*

The front of this rayon U.S. Army pillow cover from Fort Dix, New Jersey, has been damaged from the friction of repeated use. The U.S. Army insignia appears at center front above a poem dedicated "To My Wife": "A darling little Wife / Has made my dreams / come true […]." The fringe is bright yellow and the background is a less intense hue of yellow. All of the surface decoration is printed. 15.75" x 17.25". 1941-1945. $5-10. *Courtesy of Lyell D. Henry.*

This rayon U.S. Army pillow was sent from the Philippine Islands and is signed, "All My Love, Milton." Evidently, the soldier paid extra money to have the "Sweetheart" pillow cover personalized. At top center is a soldier (head only) in front of a U.S. flag. Named scenes include: 1) "Machine Gun," 2) "Para-Trooper," 3) "Tank Destroyer," 4) "Tank," 5) "Bomber," and 6) "Anti-Aircraft Gun." The poem says, "I thought that you would / like to know / That some ones thoughts / Go where you go. […]." The background is a light orange color and features pastels highlights in pink, green and blue. The fringe is blue. There is one small stain on the back. 16.25" x 15.75". 1941-1945. $10-15.

This acetate, U.S. Army pillow cover is from Camp Chaffee, Arkansas, that was renamed Fort Chaffee in 1956. In the center of a painted floral wreath of roses is an eagle, the Army's insignia, and a "To My Wife" poem: "A darling little wife / has made my dreams come true […]." This was purchased from a seller who reports that her father gave this item as a gift to her mother during World War II. This textile has never been used. 15.875" x 15.5". 1941-1945. $10-15.

A short poem for "Dear Sister" is featured on this rayon, printed "Souvenir of Canada" pillow cover with images from World War II. The poem says, "Here's a wish for happiness / in everything you do / for anything that makes you glad / will always please me, too!" Four design elements are present: 1) a shield, 2) a profile of a soldier in uniform, 3) a gun, and 4) a tank. 15.5" x 16.125". Circa 1940s. $20-30.

A bouquet of long stem roses is the predominant design on this "To My Wife," acetate pillow cover from Camp Rucker, Alabama. All surface flocking is rendered in red or green. The poem says, "A darling little wife has / made my dreams come true [...]." 16.75" x 16.625". 1942-1945. $15-20.

Chapter Five

U.S. Army Air Forces
& Souvenir Pillow Covers

On June 20, 1941, the U.S. Air Corps was incorporated into the U.S. Army Air Forces under the command of General Henry "Hap" Arnold, who served until 1946 when he was replaced by General Carl Spaatz. Both generals reported to the Chief of Staff, U.S. Army. By December 1943, this newly established branch of military service had 783 bases, stateside. By 1944, they held 80,000 aircraft. By May 8, 1945, "V-E Day" (Victory over Europe), 1-1/4 million servicemen were members. At peak size,

members numbered almost 2-1/4 million. There were 1,600 overseas locations throughout the world. The U.S. Army Air Forces was a branch of service that was in place until 1947.[1]

Inasmuch as Adolf Hitler committed suicide on April 30, 1945, the new president of Germany, Karl Dönitz, authorized the unconditional surrender of Nazi Germany to the Allies, ending Germany's part in the war.

This finished pillow from St. Petersburg, Florida, that shows planes in flight, is an extraordinary "find" because it dates from the time when the U.S. Air Force was a part of the Army. What makes it even more special is that it features a never before seen printed poem for "Daughter": "There's a song in my heart / Tis of you Daughter mine / With love thrilling thru / Every word, every line. / There's a prayer in my heart / Tis of you Daughter dear / May all gladness by yours / Every day, every year." This has a solid yellow backing. 16.75" x 16.75". 1941-1947. $25-30. *Courtesy of Beth Davis.*

Corporal Russell Murdoch Traunstein (1925-1997), from Massachusetts, served in the 15th Air Force stationed at Foggia, Italy, and later in Florence, Italy. He was a member of the 99th Bomb Group, 346th Bomb Squadron. He served as the Information and Education NCO (non-commissioned officer) to assist soldiers in discovering education and training possibilities. The Air Forces were part of the Army from 1941-1947 and gained its current name, the U.S Air Force, in October 1947.

This photo of Corporal Russell Traunstein (1925-1997) and his wife, Louise Gilbertson Traunstein (1925-) was taken on January 16, 1944, before he shipped out for duty overseas. Corporal Traunstein separated from the U.S. Army on December 7, 1945. In the meantime, he was thrilled, reportedly, when he was stationed in Florence, Italy, amid all of the great art treasures and museums! He came home safely from the war. *Courtesy of Louise G. Traunstein.*

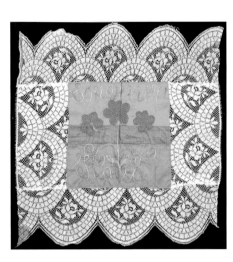

This rayon textile is decorated with orange chain-stitched flowers with yellow stems and leaves. The words "Souvenir" and "Italy" are embroidered in chain-stitch with variegated rayon thread. This is a one-layer drape to go over the back of a couch or boudoir pillow. A 5" lace border is the finishing touch. 10.125" x 10". 1944. Priceless. *Courtesy of Louise G. Traunstein.*

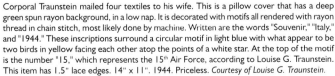

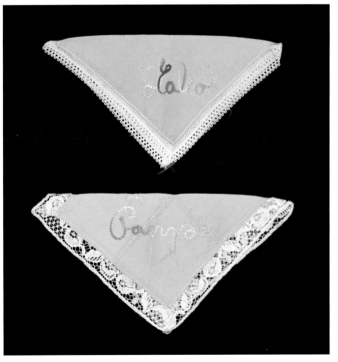

Corporal Traunstein mailed four textiles to his wife. This is a pillow cover that has a deep green spun rayon background, in a low nap. It is decorated with motifs all rendered with rayon thread in chain stitch, most likely done by machine. Written are the words "Souvenir," "Italy," and "1944." These inscriptions surround a circular motif in light blue with what appear to be two birds in yellow facing each other atop the points of a white star. At the top of the motif is the number "15," which represents the 15th Air Force, according to Louise G. Traunstein. This item has 1.5" lace edges. 14" x 11". 1944. Priceless. *Courtesy of Louise G. Traunstein.*

These two items are small, decorative souvenir handkerchiefs with writing in variegated threads, purchased in Italy by Russell Traunstein. Each has a different edge treatment. One measures 4.25" square and the other one measures 4.25" x 3.875"; both are from 1944. While every material object has some monetary value, there really is no way to place a value on irreplaceable items of great sentimental worth to the person who received them. For now, I will simply call these "priceless." *Courtesy of Louise G. Traunstein.*

This rayon World War II pillow cover that features planes and clouds in yellow flocking represents the U.S. Air Corps. It has a bright yellow fringe and a "Dearest Wife" poem: "I never dreamed / I'd go thru life / with a girl like you / my darling wife." 17" x 17.5". 1941-1945. $10-20.

Seymour Johnson was a non-enlisted, U.S. Navy test pilot who died in a plane crash in 1940. He was a native of Greensboro, North Carolina. The airfield was named for him when it opened in 1942. The site was headquarters of the Technical School of the Army Air Forces. The following years, its mission expanded to include the training of officers and cadets and training pilots in the 76th Training Wing to fly P-47 Thunderbolts. Deactivated in 1947, the base opened again in 1956.[2]

Blue and white are the overriding colors of this rayon, U.S. Army Air Forces pillow cover from Seymour Johnson Field, North Carolina. Yellow appears in an insignia and again in the fringe. A "Friendship" poem reads, "When the golden sun / is sinking / and you mind / from troubles free [...]." This is a bit wrinkled from storage, but never used. 15.75" x 16.5". Circa 1942-1947. $10-20.

This rayon pillow cover from the U.S. Army Air Forces, Atlantic City, New Jersey, is unusual for two reasons: 1) it has no fringe; and 2) it features a distinctive "Sister" verse: "Other verses may be longer / or a bit more stylish Sis - / but they can't bring / more good wishes / than were tucked away / in THIS!" This is a two-color item, and all of the letters and motifs are flocked in red. There are very slight linear stains on the backing. 16.75" x 18.375". 1941-1947. $20-25.

A large eagle and a "Remember Me" poem are the compelling images on this rayon "U.S. Air Forces" pillow cover from Victorville, California. The verse says, "When the golden sun is sinking / And you heart from care is free / When of others you are thinking ~ / Will you then remember me?" This was never used, but show a slight fading of both the yellow background (cover), and its navy blue fringe. "The U.S. Air Force" was established in October 1947. 15.25" x 16.75". 1941-1947. $5-10.

Opened in 1935, McClellan Air Force Base closed in 2001. During World War II, it is here that nearly all of the bombers that saw action in the Pacific Theater were outfitted. The base was named for Major Hezekiah McClellan (1894-1936). He received the Distinguished Flying Cross posthumously, after he lost his life while test piloting a Consolidated P-30 plane over Ohio. He is remembered for his work in charting early air routes over Alaska.[3]

This rayon, U.S. Air Forces "Mother" pillow cover, stamped with the name McClellan Field, California, is in sad shape, having been damaged in use. As on many other pillows of its kind, there are two large roses on either side of a poem which reads, "To one who bears / the sweetest name / And adds a luster / to the same [...]." There is a curious turquoise shading effect behind some of the leaves. The lettering is worn and the bottom is ripped from removal of a pillow form. Glue residue is present from a piece of masking tape on the pillow backing. 15.75" x 16.75". 1941-1945. $3-5.

On January 23, 1942, the Air Training Command (ATC) was first established as the Air Corps Flying Training Command. On July 1, 1946, its name changed from the Army Air Forces Training Command to simply the Air Training Command. The unit was headquartered at Randolph Air Force Base in Texas and its mission was to provide basic training, as well as flight and technical training. In 1993, the name of this group changed yet again.[4]

This rayon pillow cover says simply "Air Training Command." It features two planes and an insignia, which is the central motif. The fringe is navy blue. There is a light liquid stain on the front and the stain carries over to the back. Given the condition, I paid too much, sight unseen. 16.125" x 16.75". Post World War II. $3-5.

The city of Denver donated the land area that became Buckley Field, Colorado. The installation opened on July 1, 1942, as a center to train airmen aboard bombers such as the B-17 Flying Fortress and the B-24 Liberator. In addition, the site served as an area where basic training was conducted. At the time, the U.S. Army Air Forces were a part of the U.S. Army. The site was named for 1st Lieutenant John Harold Buckley (no birth or death dates available), a pilot who was killed in action during World War II in France. In October 2000, the site was renamed Buckley Air Force Base.[5]

The main design element of this U.S. Army Air Forces acetate pillow cover from Buckley Field, Colorado, is the a large emblem in the center. Against a blue background, most of the flocked letters and motif are rendered in a low loft yellow green color, the exception being a white star that features a red center circle. The bright yellow fringe is frazzled and, although worn from storage, this item seems to have never been used. 15.75" x 16.125". 1942-1945. $5-10. *Courtesy of Lyell D. Henry.*

Columbia Army Air Base in South Carolina closed in 1947. Formerly, it was called the Lexington County Airport until it was renamed in December 1941. Perhaps it is the military site remembered best for the daring pilot, James "Jimmy" H. Doolittle (1896-1993), who asked for volunteers for a secret and dangerous mission. "Doolittle's Raiders" were to engage in an air attack, using sixteen medium bombers to drop bombs on Tokyo and Nagoya, Osaka and Kobe, Japan on April 18, 1942, in retaliation for Pearl Harbor and as a wake-up call for Japan, which never expected the homeland to be attacked.

A book written by Captain Ted W. Lawson, a survivor of this mission, is titled, *Thirty Seconds Over Tokyo.* He details the events of his own plane crash into the China Sea near the island of Nantien. Severely injured, he would lose his left leg. The Chinese people were very kind to him and his crew, sheltering them, feeding them, and caring for their wounds, although medical resources were in short supply.

This acetate, U.S. Army (Air Forces) pillow cover from Columbia Army Air Base is dedicated to "Mother." Sweet words, flanked by large roses, read, "To one who bears the / sweetest name / And ads lustre [sic] / to the same […]." This item may look like it has been through a war, because it has! The pillow cover is printed on a gray background and only the base's name is flocked. This pillow cover is historically important due to its association with the Japanese air raids by "Doolittle's Raiders." 16.5" x 18.125". 1941-1947. $10-20. *Courtesy of Lyell D. Henry.*

As a quilter, I was charmed by the thought Ted Lawson was given a quilt for warmth and comfort. Later, when he was to be moved to another location in the back of a truck, three quilts were piled up for him to rest on, intended to cushion the impact of being bounced along bumpy roads. Given the extent of his injuries, the quilts did not help all that much, but those thoughtful acts of total strangers are something he appreciated.

The planes had launched from the aircraft carrier, the *U.S.S. Hornet*, which was also present at the Battle of Midway, and ultimately was sunk in the Solomon Islands, at the Battle of the Santa Cruz Islands. Once over Tokyo, the bombers targeted munitions factories and non-civilian sites, dropping sixteen tons of munitions before retreating.

The crew knew that they would run short of fuel and hoped to land on one of two Chinese airstrips that were

not occupied by the Japanese. They had no such luck. Crew members were forced to bail out with parachutes or crash. Doolittle, himself, parachuted to safety over China, along with the crews of nine other B-25 bombers. Doolittle, the person who devised this plan, lived to be ninety-six years old and was promoted to the rank of full general by President Ronald Reagan. Doolittle's obituary, written by Albin Kreeds, was published in *The New York Times* on September 28, 1993.[6]

Some crew members did not fare too well. One man died while jumping from the plane, two died by drowning as they tried to swim across a lake while under fire by the Japanese, and others were captured in China by the Japanese. Of all those "prisoners of war," three were executed for "war crimes,"[7] five were given sentences of life in prison, and one died of starvation. The Japanese did not respect the international rules set forth for humanitarian treatment, according to the Geneva Convention. The final plane landed in Vladivostok, Siberia, and was confiscated by the Soviet Union, its crew members imprisoned.

Initially called the San Antonio Aviation Cadet Center, Lackland Air Force Base was originally part of Kelly Air Force Base.

"Military Daze," a comedic pillow cover from Lackland Air Force Base, San Antonio, Texas, is a collection of five cartoons about life in the military. Clockwise, the captions say: 1) "Comes the shots… that needle always looks mighty big!" 2) "The first 2,000 miles are the hardest!" 3) "Chow time… action that beats any battlefront!" 4) "Drill practice… oops!" as two men collide, and 5) "The supply room… always a perfect fit!" (No!). This unused item shows designs on a white background, with yellow highlights. 16.5" x 1.375". Circa 1950. $25-35.

In 1948, the military training site was renamed for Brigadier General Frank Lackland (1884-1943). Known as the only U.S. Air Force military installation that conducts basic training, the "737 TRG" oversees that function. The 7,000-acre location is home to six squadrons that train airmen in certain advanced specialties. Lackland Air Force Base, in its present form, was built in 1953.[8]

September 2, 1945. The base was kept in readiness until 1953 and is currently the "Port of Ephrata," the local airport for Ephrata, Washington.[11]

This pillow cover, with the name "Drew Field, Florida," features the insignia of the Signal Corps and a poem to "Mother." The words say, "With spirit calm as the summer sea / Moving in sweet serenity […]." Drew Field was active during World War II, but renamed Tampa International Airport in 1950. Unfortunately, black residue clings to a small area of the pillow cover's front. That is probably the result of a piece of masking tape that served as a dealer's price tag. The fringe is somewhat detached on the bottom edge. 16.75" x 17.125". 1941-1950. $10-15. *Courtesy of Lyell D. Henry.*

This rayon "Mother and Dad" printed pillow cover is from Lackland Air Force Base, San Antonio, Texas. The poem says, "No one knows but Mother and Dad / about the smiles and tears we've had […]." The primary colors of this object are red, blue, and yellow. This is in mint condition. 15.375" x 17.625". Circa 1953-1970s. $25-40. *Courtesy of Lyell D. Henry.*

Drew Field covers a 160-acre land area just outside of Tampa, Florida. During World War II, the U.S. Army Air Forces renamed the site Drew Army Airfield and set up the Third Air Force there. Approximately 120,000 military men were trained there and learned to operate planes such as the B-17, C-47, AT-6, and B-25. Since 1950, it has been known as the Tampa International Airport.[9]

The Miami Beach site of the U.S. Army Air Force served as an "important Replacement Training Center for enlisted personnel in the Army Air Corps."[10]

The Ephrata Army Air Base was set up in 1942 to train crews of B-17 and B-24 bombers. Formerly, the site was used as an emergency landing strip. By 1944, the mission was extended to include the training of fighter pilots of the P-39, P-63, and P-38, a status that reverted to just training on the B-24 by the time of the unconditional surrender of Japan, signed on

This silk U.S. Army Air Force pillow cover from Miami Beach, Florida, features a "Mother" poem. All surface colors are either a rust red or leaf green, including the fringe. The poem says, "No friend half so near to me / No comrades so true / No pal half so dear to me / Mother as you. / No love half as sweet to me / No heart half so fine / As the love and the heart of you / Mother o' Mine." Large roses are present to the left of the poem, and an Air Force emblem is featured. Silk was not commonly used for textiles of this type during World War II. 15.5" x 17.125". 1942-1947. $10-15. *Courtesy of Lyell D. Henry.*

"Ephrata Air Base, Washington" are the only words on this rayon pillow cover. The background is yellow, the plane in the center is rendered in red flocking, and the letters are flocked in blue. There are small stains on the lower edge of pillow cover's backing. 15.625" x 17". 1942-1946. $20-25.

Reuben H. Fleet (1887-1975) founded a corporation called Consolidated Aircraft. In late 1935, he moved the company to San Diego. He learned to fly planes in 1917 and by 1918 he served as the "executive officer of the Army's training program."[12] By 1929, his company was the largest manufacturer of airplanes in the United States. In 1941, he sold his interests in the business. During World War II (1941-1945), the company produced more than 18,000 B-24 bombers and other planes.[13]

This "Sweetheart" pillow cover in rayon appears to have never been used. At the bottom, it defines the site of origin as "Consolidated Aircraft, San Diego, California." The distinctive poem says, "I'd like to see your sunny smile / Most any hour of the day / I'd like to visit for a while / In just the same old way. / I'd like to talk of times of yore / Just like we used to do / And feel the happiness once more / That's mine when I'm with you." Featured are various types of U.S. Army planes such as the "Lockheed," the "Douglas," the "Curtiss," and the (B-17) called the "Flying Fortress." The prominent plane shown is the B-24. 16.5" x 17". 1941-1945. This is in mint condition. $20-25.

Scott Field, near Bellville, Illinois, was named in 1917 for Corporal Frank S. Scott (1883-1912), who lost his life in a plane crash during World War I. In 1939, the site came under the aegis of the United States Army Air Corps. Today, it is called Scott Air Force Base and remains the only Air Force Base that is named for an enlisted man.[14]

In 1940, the U.S. Army Air Corps leased an airfield in Savannah, Georgia, with the intent of having it host a light bombardment group from Barksdale Field, Shreveport, Louisiana. Called "Hunter Field," the site had no permanent housing. All personnel lived in tents and 550 prisoners of war worked on the base. The site remained in operation after World War II.[15]

Chatham Army Air Field was operated in Savannah under the 3rd Air Force. By late 1944, B-29 bombers were launching from this site, and two hundred prisoners of war worked at the base. Eventually, this area became the Savannah International Airport.[16]

The vendor of this red and yellow flocked rayon U.S. Air Forces pillow cover acquired it from a World War II veteran who sent it to his fiancée when he was stationed at Keesler Field in Biloxi, Mississippi. He was there from 1944-1945. The prominent design element is a "Sweetheart" poem: "I thought that you / would like to know / That someone's thoughts / go where you go. […]." This was never used. 15.875" x 16.375". 1944-1945. $25-30.

This rayon "U.S. Air Corps" pillow cover hails from Scott Field, Illinois, and is dedicated to "Mother." Its poem says, "M is for the millions things she gave me / O means only that she's growing old […]." The images are planes, an "Anti-Aircraft Gun," a cameo of a pilot, and "The Ears of the Army." The ivory background has tinges of pink and pastel blue in a watercolor effect. Large eagle wings and a shield appear above the word "Mother." The yellow backing on this pillow could be removed as it is showing an infestation of xerophilic fungi, probably from being stored in a damp location. 15.5" x 16.5". 1939-1947. $5-10.

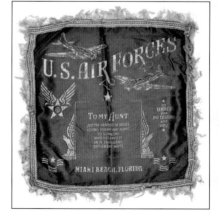

Dark tan and gray are the primary colors used to create a very special "To My Aunt" rayon pillow cover with a bright yellow fringe. This is marked "U.S. Air Forces, Miami Beach, Florida." All of the design motifs, including the poem, are flocked. Two eagles sit like bookends on either side of the poem, which says, "Just the happiest of wishes / loving you my aunt always / to someone / who deserves it / in a thousand / different ways." Additional words say, "In service to God and my country." This is a very unique and rare "Aunt" pillow and it is the only one we have ever come across. 16.625" x 16.75". 1941-1947. $20-25. *Courtesy of Lyell D. Henry.*

This rayon pillow cover comes from the Savannah Air Base, Georgia, and says "U.S. Army Air Corps" at the top. Shown are planes taking off and in the air. A "Sweetheart" poem reads, "I thought that you would / like to know / That some one's thought go / where you go, [...]." This is in excellent condition and never used. The variegated fringe features an unusual combination of colors: ivory, mint green, and rust. 16" x 16.625". 1940-1944. $40-45.

The Albuquerque Army Air Base was completed in August 1941. The first military plane to arrive was a B-18 bomber in April 1941. During the following summer, the base became very active. It hosted the 19th Bombardment Group, trained navigators for the brand new B-17 "Flying Fortress," and opened the "first wartime advanced flying school."[17] More than 2,000 pilots were on base at that time, and more than five hundred support personnel.

In February 1942, the base was renamed "Kirtland Army Air Force Base," in honor of Colonel Roy C. Kirtland (1874-1941). Recalled from retirement to once again serve his country in the Army Air Corps in 1941, Kirtland died at Moffett Field, California, at the age of sixty-five.[18]

This magenta, rayon, pillow cover with mustard yellow flocked words and designs is from Albuquerque Air Base, New Mexico, and is marked "U. S. Air Forces." A poem, "To Mother," says: "A word of love and gratitude / A little word of praise / A word to wish you happiness / In many pleasant ways / But words can never say enough / Nor wish enough it's true / The real wish is between the lines / *Dear Mother* – just for you!" 16.125" x 17.125". 1941-1942. $15-20. *Courtesy of Lyell D. Henry.*

A digitally-enhanced old Polaroid photo of my brother, John M. Grace (1943-1996), who trained at Lackland Air Force Base, has been inserted into the photo pocket of this pillow cover for "Mother." He is seen standing in front of The Alamo in this photo taken during the 1960s. If this pillow cover actually had been sent to our mother, she would have relished it! And, as it is, "Mother" is the prominent word on this acetate pillow cover from Lackland Air Force Base, Texas. The verse says, "This picture Mother / just for you / brings my love / all year through." A pretty blue, red breasted bird sits on a rose bush branch and roses can be seen next to the word "Mother." A tag says, "Picture Pillow – patent pending." This has never been used. The base was set up in 1948 and is still in operation. 16" x 17.375". 1950-1975. $10-15. *Courtesy of Lyell D. Henry.*

This rayon "Sweetheart" pillow cover from Lackland Air Force Base in San Antonio, Texas, is in top notch condition and has a tag that says simply "#10" sewn into a seam in the back of the front fringe. The words on the motif in the upper left corner say, "The Gateway to the Air Force." The words to the poem are familiar, "I thought that you / would like to know / That someone's thoughts / go where you go. [...]." 16" x 17.75". 1950-1975. $20-25.

Only three days after Pearl Harbor in December 1941, the War Department announced a decision to take over the two hundred-acre municipal airport at Walla Walla, Washington. Over $7 million dollars was spent to convert the land area into an Army Air Base. This became a training site for B-17 and B-24 ("Liberator") aircraft. In all, about 8,000 officers and enlisted men were trained and the base produced 594 heavy-bomber crews.[19]

The Amarillo Municipal Airport was taken over for military purposes early in World War II, under the control of the U.S. Air Corps. During the War, it served as a training center for new recruits, as well as engineers and mechanics who kept B-29 bombers in good repair. There were also 225 Italian prisoners of war who were put to work on the airfield. The base closed in 1968 and reverted to its former status as the Amarillo Municipal Airport.[20]

This large, flat textile is folded so that only the corner that shows the name of the base is showing. This rayon table cover in a magenta color would cover a small table, perhaps a card table. A yellow fringe surrounds its perimeter. Some creases are present from being folded for storage. The name "U.S. Army Air Forces, Walla, Walla Air Base, Washington" is present in flocked words, on just one corner. 40" x 36". 1941-1947. $20-30.

Lime green is the background color of this unusual U.S. Air Corps rayon pillow cover from Amarillo Field, Texas. A "Mother" poem in white flocked letters, within the outline of a blue star, reads (in all caps): "Tho' far away from you I seem / each night I see you in a dream / the rose long famed for its grace / is not as lovely / as your dear face / and when my work / o'er here is through / I'll hurry home to be / with you." Lime green is the background of this textile and the other decorations are flocked in red or blue. 15.375" x 17". Circa1942-1945. $5-10.

Chapter Six

Pillow Covers of the U.S. Navy

illow covers from the U.S. Navy with a "Seabee" logo are highly prized and often command a heftier than expected price at auction. The logo symbolizes the tough, brave, competent U.S. Navy engineers who functioned as a construction unit. The Seabees, a nickname for the Construction Battalions (CBs), were responsible for building "major airstrips, bridges, roads, gasoline storage tanks, and Quonset huts for warehouses, hospitals, and housing."[1]

Camp Parks, located near Livermore, California, was commissioned on January 19, 1943, as a U.S. Navy Base near San Francisco and was home to the U.S. Navy Seabees. In 1980, the site was named in honor of Rear Admiral Charles W. Parks. The facility was one of three bases in the area, collectively known as "Fleet City." Disbanded in 1946, the site was not used again until the Korean conflict. Transferred to the jurisdiction of the U.S. Army in 1959, it was renamed the Parks Reserve Forces Training Area in 1980.

The most outstanding feature of this pillow cover is its "Seabees" logo. The name, "Port Hueneme," refers to a site that was set up in May 1942 in Ventura County, California. One of its prime responsibilities was to ship equipment and goods to the Pacific arena. Seabees (CBs) were civilian recruits who were skilled tradesmen. They were placed under the command of the U.S. Navy's Civil Engineer Corps. As a group, Seabees possess an impressive record: 325,000 Seabees served on six different continents and three hundred islands during World War II.[2]

The proper noun, "Hueneme," derives from a name given by a group of Native Americans, the Chumash, to the area where the base is located. Their words, "*wene me*," translate as "resting place."[3] The land area was discovered in 1542 by Portuguese explorer Juan Rodríguez Cabrillo (1499-1543), who sailed under the Spanish flag.[4] The city was not incorporated until March 24, 1948, although its name was changed to "Port Hueneme" in 1939.[5]

This rayon U.S. Navy pillow cover from Camp Rousseau, Fort Hueneme, California, is in spectacular condition! The colors of the front of this pillow are red, blue, and yellow, and the backing is a wonderful fabric with stars showing on a navy blue background. The fringe of beige and tan yarn is quite unusual. The "Dear Sister" poem on the front says, "Do I think of you, dear / Sister! / A million times a day! / Do I love my little sister? / Much more than I can say!" A service flag with one star appears at bottom left, and an eagle at the top left stands above a shield attached to anchors. 16.25" x 17.25". 1941-1945. $40-50.

The *U.S.S. West Virginia*, "the Wee-Vee," looks deceptively peaceful on this pillow cover. On December 7, 1941, the battleship sustained the impact of seven Japanese torpedoes at Pearl Harbor. Captain Mervyn S. Bennion (1887-1941) was mortally wounded while standing on the deck when a bomb fragment scattered after hitting the center gun turret. On fire, the ship was abandoned and sank. It was not until May 17, 1942, when the ship was refloated, that the seventy bodies of trapped seamen were discovered. The ship was refurbished and used throughout the rest of the war. It was on hand at Tokyo Bay when the Japanese officially signed an unconditional agreement to surrender. The battleship was decommissioned on January 7, 1949. Subsequently, it was sold for scrap metal in 1959.[6]

This pillow cover was elegant in its day with lovely matching fringe in colors that set off the motifs on the top surface. Care was not taken in removing the pillow insert with the result that the bottom edge of the backing is torn and shredded. In better condition, textiles could command a much higher price. Take care if removing a pillow insert! Nevertheless, dating this rayon pillow is made easy! A tag sewn into the side edge and visible on top of the cover says, "Another Velvograph Product." The writing on the reverse states the copyright date as

1943 by Velvograph Co. A banner on the bottom edge of the front cover says simply, "Mother." Bedecked with seven pink or yellow roses is "U.S. Navy" at the top. The center features two battleships, overseen by an eagle, sitting upon a shield attached to anchors. This printed pillow cover has some damage to the edges. 16.75" x 16.5". 1943. $5-10.

This rayon U.S. Navy pillow cover, in complementary colors of green and red, is hand-painted with roses. Featured is the battleship the *U.S.S. West Virginia* sailing serenely on moonlit seas. In printed words, a "Sweetheart" poem reads, "I thought that you would / like to know / That someone's thoughts go / where you go. [...]." This "Wee-ve" battleship saw much action throughout World War II and was present in Tokyo Bay on September 2, 1945, when the Japanese signed the official surrender. The battleship loaned five of its musicians to the *U.S.S. Missouri* for the occasion. 16.75" x 17.25". 1941-1945. $21-30.

This pillow cover is in excellent condition and is an example of a generic U.S. Navy pillow. It is uncertain whether the artist is trying to depict sunrise or sunset, but the visual effect of the pillow calls to mind the saying, "Red sky at night, sailor's delight; red sky in morning, sailors take warning!" Yellow is the overall coloration of this acetate pillow cover with very graphic designs that are printed. At the top left is a "Friendship" poem: "Within the garden of my heart / Where flowers of friendship grow / There are blossoms of remembrance / Forget-me-nots so blue / And purple velvet pansies / To tell my thoughts of you: / And roses that will always bloom / Whatever be the weather / Whose fragrance is the memory / of days we spent / Together." At the bottom are the words, "Greetings from U.S. Navy." An eagle at the top rests on an anchor while battleships are in full view under a sunset sky. 16" x 16". 1941-1945. $10-20.

The state of Connecticut gave the U.S. Navy a land area that has 112 acres and is located along the Thames River in 1868. Officially acknowledged as a Navy site in 1871, this location has become the U.S. Navy's primary submarine base. Although it was a candidate for discontinuance in 2005, the site remains in use today.[7]

This striking U.S. Navy pillow cover in blue and yellow features the name of its site of origin, "Newport, Rhode Island," and a poem called "Remembering." The words read: "As days pass by / never feel blue / for I remember the happy times / with you / It would lighten my cares / And double my Joys / To know that you / are remembering too" (no punctuation). All of the motifs are flocked on this never used piece. Only faint fold lines are still present, so this item previously may have been lightly pressed with an iron, set on low heat. 17.125" x 17.5". 1941-1945. $60-75.

Very dramatic is this acetate U.S. Navy pillow cover from the Submarine Base of New London, Connecticut. Featured is a printed poem to "Mother and Dad," which reads, "No one knows but Mother and Dad / about the smiles and tears we've had [...]." The other surface decorations, which include two battleships, a logo, stars, and letters, are flocked. The pillow is in stellar condition. Customary fold lines are present from storage. 17.375" x 17.375". 1941-1945. $25-45. *Courtesy of Lyell D. Henry.*

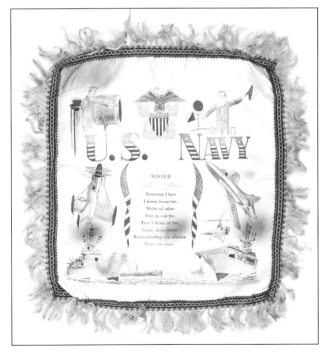

This "Sister" pillow cover from the U.S. Navy has an acetate front and a rayon back, according to a tag. Its poem reads, "Someone I love / I know loves me. / Sister of mine / true as can be. / Ever I think of the / happy days flown / Remembering you always / Sister my own." This item has been used and the edge for inserting a pillow is frayed. The fringe is matted and the backing is torn from the edges, in some places. Ships, Navy signalmen, Navy planes, and other motifs decorate this printed pillow with predominantly red, white, and blue colors. 16.125" x 17.5". Late 1950s-early 1960s. $5-10.

The name "U.S. Naval Training Center, Bainbridge, Maryland" was chosen by President Franklin D. Roosevelt in memory of Commodore William Bainbridge (1774-1833). He is perhaps best known for winning a naval battle with Great Britain's *HMS Java* during the War of 1812. Between 1942 and 1945, the training center graduated more than 244,000 recruits that went on to serve aboard naval vessels all over the world. Training at the site was discontinued in 1947, and the center was shut down for good in 1976. Many more details are available in the wiki file consulted.[9]

After the war, the United States imported a number of pillow covers made of black "spun rayon" that were manufactured in Japan. One characteristic is a shorter fringe than is usually present on most other World War II pillow covers and silver-color enhancements and lettering. The *U.S.S. Arizona* Memorial at Pearl Harbor, Hawaii, was dedicated in 1962, its visitor center opening in 1980. The ship, bombed by the Japanese on December 7, 1941, a "day that will live in infamy," is the final resting place for many of the battleship's 1,177 crew members. In 1989, it was declared a National Historic Landmark. Here it is depicted in a nocturnal scene. The background is a black spun rayon cloth that features sparkling silver highlights. There is a 1" yellow fringe all around. On the back there is both a water stain and an ink stain. This pillow cover resembles others with a known Japanese provenance. 16.5" x 16.5". Circa 1960s. $12-20.

This rayon pillow with a poem "To Mother" is from the U.S. Naval Training Center, Bainbridge, Maryland. The motifs seem to be faded, as though this item was sent to the dry cleaner, previously. The white background is printed with flowers, a shield, and a sailor, and the poem is rendered in pink lettering. Most of the design area is taken up by the poem, which is one we have not seen before: "When at morn I first awake, / My mother's eyes I see / Smiling all a-light with love / And bending over me / When the bedtime shadows fall, / I'm always sure of this, / Just as I'm drifting off to dreams, / I feel my mother's kiss." 16.25" x 7.375". 1941-1945. $15-20.

This pillow cover is from a site constructed by the U.S. Navy in 1911. During the years of the Great Depression, the base was inactive. With the announcement of the war in Europe in 1939, the site expanded. By 1945, more than 1,000 buildings were in place on 1,350 acres. The U.S. Naval Training Station, Great Lakes, Illinois, eventually became the U.S. Navy's largest training site.[8]

The top of this acetate pillow cover says, "U.S. Navy Armed Forces." Lettering at the bottom identifies it as coming from the U.S. Naval Training Station, Great Lakes, Illinois. All of the designs are flocked in blue on a white background. A blue fringe is present. This item is wrinkled, but apparently never used. 16.25" x 16.75". 1941-1945. $10-15. *Courtesy of Lyell D. Henry.*

Pastel pink and a deeper pink are the predominant colors of this rayon, "Mother and Dad" pillow cover from the "U.S. Navy," a name that is written diagonally across the textile. The abbreviation "USN" is part of an emblem with an anchor in the upper left, but roses are the main design motif. The poem says, "In all the years I've known / you both / You planned and strived / for me […]." This item looks as though it has been pressed, but was soiled at the time, and the effect is now embedded dirt. Traces of the former fold lines are still visible. Notably, this has a short 1" fringe. 16.25" x 16". 1941-1945. $7-10.

The outstanding feature of this rayon "Sweetheart" pillow from the U.S. Navy, Kodiak, Alaska, is the beautifully textured look of its background fabric. The poem, in the upper left corner, says, "I thought that you would like to know / that someone's thoughts go where you go [...]." There is a growling tiger and a large anchor. All of the words and decorations are flocked in red or blue. The backing is green, oddly enough. This is in great condition. 17" x 17". 1941-1945. $10-20.

This colorful U.S. Navy pillow cover, made of acetate, features roses that appear to be both printed and hand-painted. A poem titled "Mother O' Mine" says, "I always think of mother / No matter where I roam / I always think of mother / Although I am far from home / Friends and many others / Sometimes prove untrue / But never does a mother / For her heart is always true." This has a variegated fringe in turquoise and red. A tiny stain on the front is noted. 15.875" x 16.5". 1941-1945. $10-20.

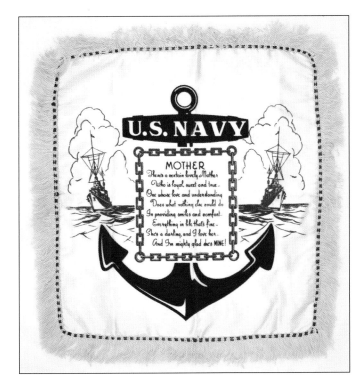

All of the decorations are flocked on this high quality, never used, rayon pillow cover from the U.S. Navy. A "Mother" poem is enclosed by "links of chain" and says, "There's a certain lovely Mother / Who is loyal, sweet and true - / One whose love and understanding / Does what nothing else could do / In providing smiles and comfort - / Everything in life that's fine - / She's a darling, and I love her - / And I'm mighty glad she's mine." A ship can be seen on either side of the poem. The main colors of the item are red, white, and blue. The overwhelming design is that of a large red anchor. There is a light turquoise color backing. The yellow fringe has navy blue highlights. 16.75" x 18.125". 1941-1945, or later. $20-25.

This rayon "Mother" pillow is in excellent condition. The color is predominantly yellow, with all other words and motifs in black, including the ships at sea, eagle with flag, poem, roses, rope, and the words, "Our Navy – America's Guardian," and an anchor with "U.S.N." The background has red and turquoise highlights added for a watercolor effect. Even the fringe is yellow. The poem says, "There's a dear little house inviting, / In a dear little place I know. [...]." 16.5" x 17". 1941-1945. $20-33.

Kaiser Ship Yards, Richmond, California, was one of four shipyards in the San Francisco Bay Area, established by Henry J. Kaiser (1882-1967). He constructed three other ship building sites. His company was established in 1939 in response to new guidelines set forth by the United States Maritime Commission. Only one of the 747 ships, the *Red Oak Victory*, produced at the Richmond Shipyards is still in existence.[10]

A photo caption found in Doris Kearns Goodwin's book *No Ordinary Time* states that with Henry Kaiser's leadership, the number of days required to produce a ship was reduced from 355 days in 1940 to 194 days in 1941 and finally, to sixty-nine days in 1942. His efforts seem to have been crucial in winning the war![11]

Five named scenes are depicted on this rayon U.S. Navy pillow cover: 1) "Heavy Cruiser," 2) "Submarine," 3) "Battleship," 4) "Destroyer," and 5) "Aircraft Carrier." A "Mother" poem decorates the center of the cover's front: "To one who bears the sweetest name / and adds a lustre [sic] to the same [...]." The designs are rendered in turquoise, yellow and red on a white background. Previously used as a pillow, this textile has stains along the back bottom edge. 16.5" x 16.5". 1941-1945. $10-15. *Courtesy of Lyell D. Henry.*

This rayon pillow cover is a "Souvenir of Kaiser Ship Yards, Richmond, California," whose motto was "Victory by Production." Stars, American flags, one large ship, and a seaside scene with battleships, as well as a shield that shows a ship in production, are the designs of this textile. Pink is the predominant color and the other designs are rendered in blue, a faint turquoise and a light tint of yellow. The turquoise backing has tiny pin-dot-size holes and one slightly larger hole as well as three small, black stains that look like ink. 15.25" x 16.5". 1939-1945. $10-15.

This early twentieth century acetate U.S. Navy pillow cover with a tan fringe has a poem to an undesignated individual: "When the golden / sun is sinking ~ And your mind / from troubles free / When of others you / are thinking / Will you sometimes / think of me?" The tan background features hand-painted roses, a ship at sea, and an eagle clutching an anchor. 16.25" x 17". Circa 1930s $25-30.

This rayon "Mother" pillow cover hails from the U.S. Navy Training Station, Sampson, New York. The steel gray background features flocked and printed images of an anchor, stars in blue, and the following poem, "To one who bears the sweetest name / And adds a luster to the same [...]." This item looks as though someone may have washed it. One edge is completely separated from the fringe at the top. 15.375" x 16.875". 1942-1945. $5-10. *Courtesy of Lyell D. Henry.*

Green is the predominant color of this rayon U.S. Navy pillow cover that features a 48-star flag and a flag with an anchor present. A large battleship appears at the bottom and in the center is an eagle grasping an American flag bunting glanced by another battleship and a biplane that has "2 MF-4" written on its side. Biplanes were mostly obsolete by the late 1930s. This item was carefully used. 15.5" x 16.125". Circa 1930s. $10-20.

This cardboard carton was used to ship the just seen "Sweetheart" pillow cover to Miss Marcella Clausen of Tracy, Iowa (in Marin County), from the Ship's Service Department, U.S. Naval Training Station, San Diego, "California," with just four 1-1/2-cent stamps ($.06 total postage).

Chapter Seven

U.S. Marine Corps, Maritime, & Merchant Marine Pillow Covers

U.S. Marine Corps

The words "The few, the proud" refer to the United States Marine Corps, initially organized on November 10, 1775. In tandem with the U.S. Navy, members of the U.S. Marines distinguished themselves during World War II in the Pacific arena. Author James Warren deems the U.S. Marines' "practice of amphibious warfare… the cornerstone of the Pacific Campaign of World War II."[1] Previously, at Guadalcanal, the Marines provided an amphibious attack on the island to prevent the Japanese from building a landing strip there. Armed with visions of Japanese atrocities, as seen in magazine photographs of the day, America's fighting men were out for revenge. The initial occupation of the island occurred on August 7, 1942, and the site was totally secured by February 9, 1943.[2] Due to perseverance and dedication, the Marines were victorious.[3]

The Marines fought bravely again in 1945 at Iwo Jima (words that mean "sulfur island") through bloody combat against hidden Japanese enemies nestled in caves underground. The battle lasted thirty-two days. During that time, there were 26,000 American casualties. The Japanese, anticipating the attack, had set up living quarters underground, complete with electricity, heat, and other amenities. Of the 22,000 Japanese who were hiding, their final casualty count numbered 21,000. Many Japanese committed suicide rather than be captured, blowing themselves up with grenades strapped to their stomachs. Others were killed when flamethrower devices were sent spiraling into the cave entrances setting them on fire. In the book, *Flags of Our Fathers*, James Bradley says, "To the general, a 'heroic fight' meant one in which all his men would die. There were no medals for survivors in the Japanese army, only for the heroic dead."[4]

This U. S. Marine Corps acetate printed "Mother" pillow cover from Parris Island, South Carolina, features a familiar poem: "To one who bears / the sweetest name / And adds a luster / to the same. [...]." The poem is enclosed by a yellow border and flanked by two roses. In the upper left is an eagle standing on the world, with an anchor fixed in place in the background. The eagle carries a banner that says *Semper Fidelis*," which means "Always Faithful," the slogan of the Marine Corps. A light red or rust color fringe completes the item. This is in mint condition, although slight folds lines are visible. 16.75" x 17.5". Circa 1950s. $20-30.

On February 23, 1945, to boost morale, an American flag attached to a metal pole was raised by six men — Hank Hansen, Boots Thomas, Harold Schrier, Louis Charlo, Jim Michaels, and Chuck Lindberg — near the top of the volcano at Iwo Jima. Deemed too small, that particular flag was taken down and a call was sent out for a larger American flag that would be easier to see from afar. A second flag-raising that same day received so much publicity the first flag-raising event was all but forgotten.

An action photo of the second flag-raising, taken by Joe Rosenthal, *Associated Press*, touched the hearts of Americans as soon as it hit the mainstream American press. Considered to be the most widely known photograph from World War II and one of the most famous of all time, the photo shows five Marines and one Navy Corpsman as they struggle to raise "Old Glory" atop Mount Suribachi. The photo is titled "Flag Raising on Iwo Jima."

Myths and Misunderstandings

Later, a myth would circulate that the Rosenthal photo was "posed," a misinterpretation of an answer that Joe Rosenthal gave to a reporter's question. A photo taken later in that same day, with a larger group of Marines and the flag, had, indeed, been posed.

Another misunderstanding that surrounded Rosenthal's famous photo involves a false name report provided by Rene Gagnon when asked for a list of names of the flag-raisers. He identified one of the men as "Hank Hansen," yet Harlon Block's own mother claimed to have recognized her son immediately in the photo, although the shot was taken from behind! Later, the Marine was correctly identified as Harlon Block. In the meantime, it took an eighteen-month Congressional investigation to clear up the matter.

The names of the men who were involved in the second flag-raising are: Harlon Block, Mike Strank, Franklin Sousley, Ira Hayes, John Bradley, and Rene (pronounced "Rainy") Gagnon. Some problems would arise for these instant "heroes." Upon seeing the photo, President Roosevelt ordered that all six men be relieved of combat duty immediately to come home and help raise money for the war effort through the 7th War Bond drive. There was a critical need to raise money to continue the financing the war. In a twist of fate, by the time Roosevelt's wishes were pronounced, three of the men — Franklin Sousley, Michael Strank, and Harlon Block — had been killed in battle and "Doc" Bradley, a medic, had been injured and evacuated from the island, leaving only Ira Hayes and Rene Gagnon to the task at hand.

To complicate matters, Ira Hayes threatened to kill Rene Gagnon if he revealed his identity as one of the flag-raisers because Hayes did not want to sell war bonds. Gagnon was forced to reveal Hayes' identity at a Senate committee meeting. When they eventually met again, face to face, Hayes was cool toward Gagnon and virtually non-communicative.

The Battle of Iwo Jima was hardly over when the scene atop Mount Suribachi was captured on film, but for a moment in time, there was a small break in the war when all could cheer the colors of the homeland. The book, *Flags of Our Fathers*, provides a study of the lives of each of the six men who were involved with the second flag-raising. John Bradley said his father, the book's author James Bradley, did not consider himself a hero. Upon returning home, he assumed a quiet life as a funeral director and family man. He never went out of his way to discuss the war with either the press or his own family. He believed that the true heroes were the soldiers who did not leave Iwo Jima alive. The memory of the condition in which he found his best friend, Iggy, murdered by the Japanese, haunted the rest of his days.

On a parallel to the poems found on "Sweetheart" or "Mother" pillows, consider the words that Franklin Sousley wrote on the back of a photograph given to his mother. He was one of the flag-raisers who did not come home. He wrote, "To the kindest friend I ever knew, / the one I told all my troubles to. / You can look the world over, but you won't find another / like you, my dear Mother." He signed the message, "Love, Franklin."[5]

On the home front, Senator Joseph O. Mahoney of Wyoming proposed production of a three-cent postage stamp to carry the image of Rosenthal's photo and, in 1945, 150 million stamps of this kind were published. Based on the photo, a large bronze statue, the largest in the world at five stories high, was designed by Felix de Weldon and erected outside the walls of Arlington National Cemetery in Virginia. The words on the statue say, "In honor and memory of the men of the United States Marine Corps who have given their lives to their country since 10 November 1775. Uncommon valor was a common virtue." In 2005, a year that commemorated the 230th anniversary of the Marine Corps, an Iwo Jima silver dollar that features Rosenthal's photo was minted.

This pillow cover was formerly owned by a woman Marine described by the seller as "a Molly Marine." Unfamiliar with the term, I discovered through an online search that "Molly Marine" is the name of a statue that was sculpted by Enrique Alferez, a former map maker for Pancho Villa during the Mexican Revolution, that he provided free of charge, as a tribute to all women in the service. The original statue was dedicated on November 16, 1943, and stands near the French Quarter in New Orleans, Louisiana. Two copies of the statue were erected: one at the Quantico Marine Reservation, Virginia, and one at Parris Island, South Carolina.[6]

An online seller, who acquired this item from an estate, theorizes that perhaps this Molly Marine purchased the pillow cover for a sister, but never gave it to her. It is known that the woman served during World War II and retired in 1970 as a Master Gunnery Sergeant. She attended boot camp at Parris Island, South Carolina.

Believing an advertisement that stated that pillow covers from the U.S. Marine Corps are rare, I probably paid more than I should have for this rayon textile that is missing a lot of its flocking and exhibiting some color mutation on the lower edge. Keep the word "condition" in mind whenever purchasing a vintage pillow cover. 16.75" x 17.75". 1941-1945. $15-20.

A "Sister" poem graces this acetate printed pillow cover from the U.S. Marine Corps site at Parris Island, South Carolina: "Of all the Girls / I ever knew, / There never was / One like you / You're the nearest / You're the dearest / Pal I ever knew." A large eagle straddling a flag and the Marine logo plus a spray of roses and other yellow flowers are featured. The pillow backing is of an unusually stiff and sturdy texture. There is slight color mutation on the background, at the front bottom, from blue to light lavender, a change that may have occurred through the application of heat from an iron. 17.125" x 16.875". 1943-1970 (dates of Marine service of this item's previous owner). $25-30.

This rayon U.S. Marine Corps pillow cover looks elegant in its simplicity. On a bright blue background are the words "United States Marines" in red flocking, and the emblem of the Marines in yellow and white flocking. The fringe is yellow. The words *Semper Fidelis* are clearly visible as they appear on a banner trailing from an eagle's beak. This has four fold lines and has been used. 16.375" x 17.25". 1941-1945. $50-55. *Courtesy of Lyell D. Henry*

This U.S. Marines rayon printed "Sweetheart" pillow cover holds a mystery. Its poem says, "I thought that you would / like to know / That some one's thoughts go / where you go. […]." A black permanent marker blots out a name previously included on the front of the pillow. The name is not at all visible. We can only speculate about this situation. Named images include: 1) "Rifle Range," 2) "World War Monument," 3) "New Barracks," 4) "Salute Battery Dock," 5) "Headquarters & Lyceum," 6) "Ribault Monument," and 7) "Inspection – Guard of Honor." The predominant colors are yellow and pink. A price tag on the back, written on masking tape, says $3.75. The pillow cover is in excellent condition. 15.125" x 16.25". Post 1945. $20-30. *Courtesy of Lyell D. Henry.*

The anthem of the U.S. Marine Corps is celebrated on this blue, red, and yellow acetate pillow cover with an ochre fringe: "From the halls of Montezuma / to the shores of Tripoli / we fight our country's battles / on the land as on the sea / first to fight for right and freedom / and to keep our honor clean / we are proud to claim the title of United States Marines." An action scene involving Marines is shown on this textile from Parris Island, South Carolina. A "Mother" poem says, "To one who bears the sweetest name/ and adds a lustre [sic] to the same […]." This item is in excellent condition. 16.75" x 17.5". 1941-1945. $15-20.

A never-before-seen poem graces the front of this acetate U.S. Marines pillow cover from Parris Island, South Carolina, with a pink fringe: "My Dear Wife": "From memory's garden I recall / The sweetheart days we knew, / With lovely flowers, singing birds, / And skies of azure blue. / Dear Wife of Mine, how sweet / the words, / A hoped for dream come true, / My heart is happy when I think / Of home sweet home, and You." The set-up for this pillow cover is similar to others we have seen from Parris Island, with a Marine symbol, roses, and a yellow border surrounding the poem. A liquid stain on the bottom edge of the pillow cover diminishes its value. 16.5" x 18". Circa 1950s. $10-15. *Courtesy of Lyell D. Henry.*

U.S. Maritime Service

The U.S. Maritime Service was responsible for training Merchant Marines. Unlike the U.S. Marines Corps, the Merchant Marines were not a branch of the armed services. Instead, it was a group of civilians who signed on to guard a specific ship for one or two years, and to work in whatever capacity was needed. Some of the men had disabilities that would have precluded them from joining another branch of the service.

The United States Maritime Service was established in 1938 in accordance with an Act of Congress in 1936. Its purpose was to train the officers and crews of Merchant Marine vessels. When the involvement of the United States in World War II seemed inevitable, the Maritime Commission began building battleships and "Liberty Ships." By 1945, 2,700 Liberty Ships had been constructed. After the war, the United States Maritime Service disbanded and the officers were absorbed into other branches of service.[7]

During World War II, the private shipping industry was in much danger from torpedoes, bombs, and kamikaze attacks from military vessels. Loss of life by members of the Merchant Marines was exceeded only by that of the United State Marine Corps.[9]

Yellow is the riveting background color of this rayon "Mother" pillow cover from the U.S Maritime Service that features four large roses and a seal. The poem says, "To one who bears the sweetest name / and adds lustre [sic] to the same [...]." This item came with the return address of a sailor at the USMS Training Station, Sheepshead Bay, New York, and an envelope with a three-cent "Win the War" postage stamp. The fringe has separated from the pillow top on the left side for a length of five inches. This has never been used. 15.75" x 16.5". 1941-1946. $10-15.

This rayon pillow cover bears the seal of the "United States Maritime Service" and is covered with red stars, lettering, and a large ship, all printed on a dull, gray background. The backing is equally dull, and the pillow appears to have been used, if stains are any indication. Nonetheless, this is a rare item. This is one of a set of ten Merchant Marine pillows that the seller indicates he went to a lot of trouble and time to collect. 16.125" x 15.25". 1941-1945. $10-15.

Santa Catalina Island, which is located just twenty-two miles south-southwest of Los Angeles, was closed to tourists during World War II, preempted for the war effort. Local steamships were commandeered to transport troops and the island was occupied by the U.S. Coast Guard, U.S. Army Signal Corps, U.S. Navy, and U.S. Maritime Service, which all established training sites there. In addition, the Office of Strategic Services (a forerunner of the Central Intelligence Agency) occupied the island.[8]

This rayon U.S. Maritime Service pillow cover from Catalina Island, California, is colorful with its bright yellow background and crossed American flags. The colors are a combination of yellow, red, and blue. This has many light stains, and the loops of the fringe are loose in some places. 16.875" x 17.875". 1941-1945. $5-10.

Approximately 7,000 U.S. Merchant Marines were killed during World War II on more than eight hundred ships that sank. Although the mariners were subject to military regulations, they were not awarded the same benefits because they were a civilian organization. Congress finally passed a law in 1988 granting members of the Merchant Marines "veteran status." By then, 125,000 people, half of the individuals who had served, already were deceased.[10]

This acetate pillow cover has an interesting background fabric with a ribbed weave. The words "United States Maritime Service" appear on a seal that has an anchor motif. The name can be seen again at the top of the pillow cover. All of the designs on the pink-orange background are flocked in an indigo blue color. Included is a "Mother" poem: "With spirit calm as the / summer sea / Moving in sweet serenity [...]." The backing of this never used item is a yellow green. 16.25" x 15.25". 1938-1945. $14-20.

This acetate World War II pillow cover shows the following words or motifs in navy blue on a light gray background: 1) The U.S. Maritime seal, 2) a ship at sea, 3) stars, and 4) "U.S. Maritime Service." The simplicity of this item is charming. It was never used as a pillow. 15.5" x 15.5". 1941-1945. $20-30.

Two colors only are used to create the front of this rayon "U.S. Maritime Service" pillow cover. All of the letters and designs are offered in yellow flocking and include the United States Maritime Seal, a ship at sea, and stars. The background is light turquoise and the pillow cover seems to have never been used. 16.25" x 15.75". 1938-1945. $10-15.

Red is the background color of this rayon U.S. Merchant Marine pillow cover from St. Petersburg, Florida. Pink and gray flocking are used to make the other designs, including large roses. Featured is a "Mother and Dad" poem (all in caps): "You're the very best couple / that ever was paired / whatever was given / alike you have shared / many more years / may your hearts be made glad / and may your blessings be many / dear Mother and Dad!" 15.75" x 17". 1941-1945. $10-15.

This acetate pillow cover with the words "Merchant Marine" features a globe, a ship at sea, roses, and an unusual "Mother" poem. The capitalized words say, "A word of love and gratitude / a little word of praise / a word to wish you happiness / in many pleasant ways / but words can never say enough / nor wish enough, it's true / the real wish is between the lines / dear Mother – just for you!" This has an ivory and magenta (variegated thread) fringe. This has been used. Some of the flocking has worn off and there are stains on the backing fabric. 17" x 16.75". 1941-1945. $5-10.

The eagle on this acetate U.S. Merchant Marine pillow cover has his arms raised in a "V" for "Victory" sign. Two large red roses flank both sides of a brief "Sister" poem: "Of all the girls I ever knew / There never was one like you [...]." The background of this pillow is ivory in color. 16.75" x 16". 1938-1945. $10-15.

A rayon "Mother" pillow cover from the United States Merchant Marine has a yellow-tan background and motifs in red and blue flocking. The poem says, "You are the sweetest Mother / in the world for you we / keep our flag unfurled / It gives us courage way out / here to know you're waiting / Mother Dear." The line breaks of the poem are located in the most unlikely places! Other writing includes the Latin phrase "*Acta non Verba*," which means "Act, Don't Talk." 16.5" x 16.75". 1941-1945. $10-20.

Chapter Eight

Other Related Textiles

This pillow quilt is a composite of twenty pillow covers made of rayon or acetate from many different branches of the Armed Services, all sewn together to provide a patriotic and colorful display. Needless to say, it would be impractical to attempt to use this textile as a bed quilt. This item is in excellent condition. 64.125" x 85.125". 1941-1945. $250-350.

No one knows who first conceived of the notion of sewing a number of pillow covers together to create a larger textile. Each textile will be described here.

Top Row

· On the far left, is a U.S. Navy pillow cover with a Navy blue background, yellow flocked words and designs, and a ship at sea. The "Sweetheart" pillow says, "Love unending / warm and true / Sweetheart mine this / brings to you […]."

· Second from left is a "Fort Knox, Kentucky" pillow cover with the words, "The Armored Forces." The image of a large eagle carrying both olive branches and arrows in its talons and the depictions of armored tanks are flocked in a yellow color on a white background. This is a simple, yet effective, design. Notations on the back include: "333572124, 466th Bomber Group, 784th Bomb Squadron, Alamogordo, New Mexico."

· Third from left is this pillow cover in yellow with red flocking. It celebrates the U.S. Army "Paratroops" stationed at Fort Bragg, North Carolina. The back of the pillow cover has the following notations: "513th Parachute Infantry Band, A.P.O. #333, 190th Glider."

· On the far right is a U.S. Marine Corps pillow cover from New River, North Carolina. The customary Marine logo is in the center and the usual stars and shields seen on other textiles of this type are also present.

Second Row

· Far left is a "Friendship" pillow cover from Camp Pickett, Virginia, that is light apricot in color and has various printed scenes, including a plane, paratroops, and an anti-aircraft gun. The poem reads: "Oh the world is wide / and the world is grand / and there is little / or nothing new / But the finest thing / is the / Grip of the hand / of a friend that is / tried and true." The written notation on the back of this pillow cover says, "110th Infantry Band."

· The pillow cover second to left is from the U.S. Air Forces, Clovis, New Mexico. The words say, "In service for my country and you." A "Sweetheart" poem, surrounded by Eagles sitting like bookends, has these words: "There's no one else / in this world / so wonderful, charming / and so thoughtful too / There's no one else / in this world / I could love like you / my sweetheart." The rose color background is very attractive and the white and yellow flocking is very pretty. The notation on this pillow cover's back is "355th Bomb Squadron / A.A.B."

· Third from left is a U.S. Army Air Forces, Atlantic City, New Jersey, pillow cover. The overall coloration is red (flocking) on a white background. A "Sweetheart" poem says, "Love unending / warm and true. / Sweetheart mine this / brings to you […]." The banner at the top is stylized to look like a ribbon, blowing in the breeze. Simple lines, shapes, and stars complete this graphic design. The back has a handwritten notation that says, "709th Tri Group A.A.F. – T.T.C., 74th Training Wing A.A.F.-T.T. C., Squadron A, Room 175."

· The pillow cover on the far right is from the U.S. Naval Air Station, Corpus Christi, Texas. The images are in pastel hues, set on a light pink background. "U.S. Navy" is written in deep rose color script, encircled by two lines of rope with anchors on the each end. These emanate from an eagle motif standing on a shield at the top center of the pillow. Printed images include an "aircraft carrier, a destroyer, a battleship, a submarine, and a heavy cruiser." The back of this pillow cover simply says, "Yardcraft."

Third Row

· On the far left pillow cover, a large anchor with the letters "USN" superimposed on it rests in the center. The words, in blue and white lettering, are simple: "United States Navy" and "Training Station, Sampson, New York."

· Second from left, this pillow cover is from the United States Army Air Forces' Maxwell Field, Alabama, site. The light orange

color background is complementary to the blue center circle that contains an insignia. The notation on the back says, "Squadron K9, Cl. 44C, A.A.F.P.F.S. (Pilot)."

· Gray is the background of choice for the next pillow cover. This states simply, "U.S. Air Forces." Two large roses flank a poem titled, "Remember Me," which says, "When the golden / sun is sinking / and you heart / from care is free […]."

· The final image, to the far right, is an Army Air Force pillow cover from Keesler Field, Mississippi, with printed motifs and a predominantly ochre and pink color background combination. A "Sweetheart" poem – one we already have seen often – begins: "I thought that you / would like to know / that someone's thoughts / go where you go […]." Featured are seven images of planes. The notation on the back says, "Flight A 563 T.S.S. – 571."

Fourth Row

· The "U.S. Army Air Forces" pillow cover, on the far left, is totally flocked in a deep yellow color that looks elegant on a warm gray background. Featured is the poem, "Remembering," which says, "As days pass by I never feel blue / for I remember the happy times with you / It would lighten my cares / and double my joys / to know that you are remembering too."

· The second pillow is from the U.S. Marine Corps. A poem titled "To My Wife" says, "A darling little Wife / has made my dreams come true /She blesses all my life / Her name is only You […]." Again, two large roses on either side of the poem seem to be a favorite motif on many pillow covers.

· Yet another U.S. Air Forces "Sweetheart" pillow cover, hailing from Kearns, Utah, is included in this composite textile. The poem is familiar by now, "I thought that you would like to know / That someone's thoughts go where you go […]." The background is a medium yellow while the writing and other motifs are flocked in an Indigo blue.

· On the far right, planes going up into the sky form the "V" for "Victory" sign in this United States Navy pillow cover from their "Training Station, Sampson, New York." A "PT" boat and a battleship are also shown. All motifs are flocked. The eagle motif has been damaged by some sharp object, and there is a sticky splotch of glue, or other substance, near the bottom of the shield.

Fifth Row

· Far left, this U.S. Air Forces pillow cover from Greensboro, North Carolina, in deep Navy blue, with light gray flocked letters and motifs, features a unique poem that we have not seen on other covers. It is printed with all of the letters capitalized and has two titles: "Sweetheart" and "Remember Me." It says, "It is sweet to be remembered / when you're feeling sad / and blue / it sets the pulse a-throbbing / and it cheers the heart up too / It makes the world worth / living / to be remembered just by / you."

· A tan and orange pillow cover from U.S. Army Camp Pickett, Virginia, is quite distinctive due to its coloration and its poem for "Sweetheart": "Just in case you might / be lonesome / This will show / I'm lonesome, too. / But more proud / than ever Sweetheart, / That my love / belongs to you!"

· The third pillow cover, from the left, is one with a brown background and yellow and red flocked letters and motifs. This one is from the U.S. Air Forces, Greensboro, North Carolina. Its "Sweetheart" poem says, "There's no one else / in this world / so wonderful, charming / and so thoughtful too / There's no one else / in this world / I could love like you / my sweetheart."

· The final pillow cover on this composite spread has a Navy blue background and deep yellow, flocked letters and designs. This one is from the "Naval Training School," Keystone Schools (Radio). This pillow cover looks especially nice because it is set off by a fringe that has been attached to the total perimeter of this quilt. The yellow color of the fringe mimics the deep, almost gold-color of the cover's design motifs.

Not Just Pillow Covers...

Other very interesting textiles show up from both World War I and World War II. Among these are three flat textile panels that are small and meant to hang vertically from a metal attachment. These unique items were collected by Lyell D. Henry and appear to be British in origin.

Pillow pouches were given as gifts to "Mother" or "Sweetheart" during both wars. These sentimental souvenirs of war or geographical locations often feature a poem. The "pouch" inside could be used to keep letters, lingerie (very dear in times of war), or handkerchiefs.

These two textile banners from World War I, fiber content unknown, are very similar. The flags of Great Britain and Canada are featured and say: "One with Britain ~ Heart and Soul." The designated area for affixing a photo has simulated printed photo "corners" as a person would find in an early twentieth century photo album. Other motifs are the British crown and Canada's maple leaves, as well as a soldier with a gun. The banner, with an orange background, measures 9.75" x 12.625". The other one, with a dark green background, measures 9.625" x 12.75". 1917-1918. Textiles such as these are not seen on the market today and, therefore, it is difficult to assign a price. *Courtesy of Lyell D. Henry.*

Inside this World War I collectible is featured a "Just Hello" poem: "I'd like to be with you a while and hear about / the folks, / I'd like to sit and see you smile at the same / old jokes. / But since you are so far away I cannot hope to / go. / I'll send along this little token, just to say / Hello." Lady Liberty is seen holding an American flag to the left of the poem and a doughboy with a rifle stands in front of a shield, just under a large eagle, to the right. The inside pouch is formed by a piece of silk printed with the American flag. The pillow cover has a small appliquéd scene of a flag and a cannon and features the words, "Forget me not."

The interior of the pouch is silk and must have been even more beautiful when it was new. The recipient of this lovely World War I treasure is most likely no longer with us. A person can only wonder how this item was used.

A third similar textile with a medium blue background appears to have come from the same manufacturer. The textile panel lacks the image of a soldier but retains the flags of Canada and Great Britain. A lion sits under the words "Honor Bound" and a more stylized shape with curved edges encloses the space to attach a photo. 9.625" x 12.875". 1917-1918. Priceless. *Courtesy of Lyell D. Henry.*

A silk blue "Forget Me Not" pouch from World War I has a printed date of 1917 and was copyrighted by the "SP & N Company, New York." The copyright notice is so small that it is barely visible, even with a magnifying glass. Its elegant lace and trim and beautiful silk embroidered panel on the front is reminiscent of the silk embroidery work done by the French. This pouch would have made a lovely gift to a mother, sweetheart, sister, wife, aunt, grandmother, daughter, or friend. 12.25" x 9.375". 1917. $25-30.

The next four photos depict the exteriors and interiors of two World War II collectible pouches, for "Mother" and "Sweetheart."

When this rayon World War II hanky or letter pouch is folded closed, a person can see a hand-painted rose, the word "Mother," and an eagle atop an American flag shield. Inside, an American flag design forms a pocket, and the name "Hugh" is written in pencil. If opened flat, this pouch measures 9.5" x 14.125". 1941-1945. $30-40.

This "Sweetheart" pouch features a hand-painted rose design on the cover and the country of Puerto Rico. The Jones-Shafroth Act, passed by Congress and signed into law by President Woodrow Wilson on March 2, 1917, gave citizenship to Puerto Rican nationals and made them eligible for the draft. Puerto Ricans served in both World War I and II. 9.75" x 14". 1941-1945. $30-40.

Inside the front flap, there is a poem: "Each petal represents a flower / Each bud a kiss for you / Each stem an arm entwined about / My mother, dear and true."

Inside the flap is a poem, enclosed by an elaborate square with a rose in each corner, that says, "I thought that you would like to know / that someone's thoughts go where you go. / that someone never can forget / the hours we spent since first we met, / That life is richer sweeter far / For such a sweetheart as you are / And now my constant prayer will be / That God may keep you safe for me." The interior bottom pouch shows an ocean side scene of Puerto Rico, with a hut, swaying palm trees, a sailboat and a fortress built in 1539 by Spanish settlers called the Fort San Felipe del Morro, or simply, "El Morro." The old citadel that protected Puerto Rico from sea attacks is situated in San Juan.

Chapter Nine
Care and Storage of Pillow Covers

The pillow covers featured in this book are made of silk, wool, rayon, or acetate. Design elements are printed, embroidered, hand-painted, or flocked. Any cleaning, pressing, or storing of these items will be dictated by the types of fibers they hold. The first challenge for novice collectors is to identify the materials used to make each pillow cover, in part to be able to know which type of archival tissue to purchase for the purpose of storage.

Gaylord Bros., an archival supply company, offers the consumer two kinds of acid free tissue paper and acid free storage boxes. Buffered tissue is treated with calcium carbonate to increase its pH level to 8.5 (7.0 is neutral). It is thicker and less pliable tissue than unbuffered tissue. Buffered tissue is recommended for wrapping cotton or linen items. Both cotton and linen have cellulosic fibers, as they are derived from plant sources. For storage, rayon can be treated like cotton, as its composition includes processed cotton linters. By the way, as the first man-made fiber, rayon is not a synthetic, unlike other man made cloth such as polyester or nylon.

Various fibers require different kinds of care. If the pillow cover you have is made of silk, wool, or leather (whose fibers are products of animal sources), or if a textile contains unknown fibers, unbuffered tissue should be used for wrapping. Unbuffered tissue is pH neutral and thinner and, therefore, a better candidate for interleaving textiles.

Most people have little trouble in determining certain types of textiles by sight and feel. After all, natural fibers, i.e. cotton, linen, wool, and silk, are used to make clothing.

Keep in mind that rayon is by far the predominant fabric used in World War II pillow covers. For the most part, it is recognizable by its bright sheen and fully saturated colors. Rayon can appear less lustrous if it has undergone a de-lustering process. Rarely, a tag on the pillow cover will reveal its fiber content. It is not uncommon for rayon pillows to have an acetate backing.

One simple way to determine basic fiber content is to conduct a burn test. Use tweezers or a hemostat to hold fibers over a flame. Cotton smells like burning paper and leaves an ash residue. Fibers that contain animal protein (silk or wool) will smell like burning hair. Polyester fibers will smell like chemicals and the fibers will melt rather than turn to a dusty ash.

If a person wants to be very accurate in determining fiber content, I suggest using a microscope to view a loose, gathered strand of fiber, perhaps removed from an interior seam of a pillow cover. A new website, "The Fiber Reference Image Library" or "FRIL" (https://fril.osu.edu), was developed with grant money from the National Park Service and the National Center for Preservation Technology. Eventually, it will include examples of all kinds of plant fibers, animal fibers, and man-made fibers for comparative study by the general public. Any questions about the project should be directed to Kathryn Jakes, professor, Ohio State University, College of Education and Human Ecology.

The late Virginia Stevens of Contoocook, New Hampshire, a weaver and embroiderer, once gave me the following advice, from a layman's point of view: "Under a microscope, cotton looks like twisted ribbon; wool resembles hair follicles, and its rough surface makes it easy to spin; rayon looks like spaghetti; and linen looks like bamboo shoots."

Rayon

Rayon pillow cases were sold as items that were folded flat. The reason for that is so that they could be easily mailed. Unfortunately, rayon fibers hold a crease very well. Many pillow covers sold today have deep, set-in creases from being stored for decades, usually folded in fourths. Light stretching by placing an appropriate size pillow insert inside the pillow cover may help diminish those crease lines over time.

Steaming may be another option to relax wrinkles in pillow covers, but be ever cautious if choosing this method. For those pillow covers that are decorated with flocked letters and designs, do not attempt to steam them. Flocking is a technique in which short fibers are adhered to a textile background with a fixative, in the same manner used to create pennants. Steam will release the fibers from the adhesive used to apply them.

Rather than use an iron to create steam, it is more ideal to use a steam machine intended for home use. Hold the steam wand about ten to twelve inches above the surface of the object and use cool steam. Use your fingers to very lightly smooth the textile to release the tension held in the age-old wrinkle. Theoretically, a steam iron could be adapted for this purpose. However, most people use an iron to press their clothing and are used to adding tap water to the iron's water reservoir. This water may contain minerals that can spurt out, without notice, staining whatever you hope to press.

The following advice applies only to rayon pillow covers. Wiggle the pillow cover opening onto a smaller ironing board meant for sleeves. If you choose to apply the heat of a dry iron, turn the pillow cover inside out to press it from the wrong side. Dampen a piece of muslin with a water spritzer that contains distilled water. The dampened muslin should be larger than the sole plate of the iron. Place the press cloth directly on the crease and use an up and down motion to apply heat to an area that you have smoothed out beforehand. Rayon must be pressed at a low heat setting, #3 on my iron.

The outside flap of some envelopes in which some of these pillow covers were mailed state that they could be pressed with a warm iron. Always keep in mind that there is a difference between "pressing" (an up and down, light motion) and ironing (which has lots of movement, heat and pressure). Press, but do not "iron," these pillow covers!

Although wet-washing is not an option for cleaning rayon pillow covers at home, the process can be attempted in a textile cleaning laboratory under controlled circumstances. Wet rayon fibers become temporarily weak and prone to damage when handled, losing forty to seventy percent of their textile strength.[1] The danger of damaging the textile while it is wet is ever present. Applying any detergent to rayon will leave a residue that can promote further growth of conidia (fungi spores).

Dry cleaning will present its own issues. I received a U.S. Army pillow cover that smelled awful, usually an indication of an active mold colony. It was covered with an unknown white substance that looked like mold. Not wanting to keep an infested item on hand, I had no other alternative than to bring it to the dry cleaner. There, I was required to sign a disclaimer that I would not hold the business responsible if the result was not satisfactory. The textile was essentially ruined by dry cleaning.

According to mycologist Mary-Lou Florian, the word "fungi" is a scientific term. "Mold" and "mildew" are common names. She states, "Mildew is often used to refer to a group of plant pathogens. The most important

point is to determine why they (the objects) are infested with fungi." She cites the most common cause as high humidity and explains that if there is enough moisture on the surface of the textile, that condition can support fungal growth. She adds, "The fungi grow black strands (hyphae)." These can infiltrate "the fiber structure and be impossible to remove."[2]

Acetate

Acetate, developed by Camille and Henri Dreyfus in Switzerland, has different properties than rayon. Though acetate contains cellulosic fibers like rayon, it is stronger when wet. Stains such as "fruit, tea, coffee and beverages" can be removed with soap and water.[3] Tepid or lukewarm water should be used and cleaning should be very gently done. Acetate pillow covers should be air-dried, not placed in a dryer. They can be pressed on the wrong side of the fabric on the lowest heat setting your iron provides. Before wet-washing, please be certain that a tag verifies that the pillow cover is 100% acetate, front and back.

~~~~~

The following photos provide visual information regarding fungal growth on pillow covers.

This is the first pillow cover that I sent to be dry cleaned. The name "Fort Sam Houston, Texas" is its primary design element. The Fort was named for Sam Houston, the first president of the Republic of Texas. The Fort was founded in 1876 and has served as the primary training location for Army medical staff since the end of World War II.

This rayon U.S. Army pillow cover from Fort Sam Houston, San Antonio, Texas, was full of mildew when I received it. In an attempt to "save" it, I enlisted the help of a dry cleaner. This is one of two pillow covers that I chose to dry clean, as a last resort. The process left two results: 1) most all of the yellow flocking was removed, leaving only faint traces of the poem and designs, and 2) the color turquoise now has been added to the yellow fringe, in places, teaching the lesson that rayon will easily absorb colors when placed in a dry cleaner's vat. The soiled areas are no longer present.

The "Sweetheart" poem said: "There is no one else / in this world / so wonderful, charming / and thoughtful too / there's no one else / in this world / I could love like you / my sweetheart." 16.25" x 18.75". 1941-1945. The actual price $17.25, and dry cleaning added $6.80. This item has no resale value.

This pillow cover suffered ink loss when it was dry cleaned. In a laboratory situation, the ink could be covered with wax, temporarily, to prevent a loss of the printed colors, according to Margaret T. Ordoñez, professor at the University of Rhode Island, Textiles, Fashion Merchandising and Design Department in Kingstown, Rhode Island.[4] She is in charge of the university's "Textile Conservation Laboratory."

This U.S. Army pillow cover is covered with mold on the back. If one looks closely at the photo, one can see a brownish-blackish tint of color behind the poem. That is mold. Sometimes, if mold is present only on the back, the backing can be carefully removed, and the front treated with heat from a hair dryer, if one takes proper health precautions.

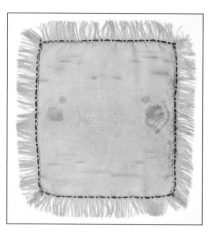

This rayon pillow cover represents the second sacrificial experiment to see whether dry cleaning could remove mold and what other effects might result. As you can see, the beautiful images are completely washed out, and yet the black staining from mold/ mildew clings to both the front and back of the pillow cover. This textile features a "Mother" poem: "M is for the million things she gave me / O means only that she's growing old […]." Featured are ships at sea, an eagle with a bunting sitting at top center, and a yellow fringe, also stained from mold. 15.25" x 17". $6.80 to have the item dry-cleaned. No resale value due to condition. *Courtesy of Lyell D. Henry.*

This is what the back of the same pillow looks like, after having it professionally dry cleaned.

On this rayon U. S. Army pillow cover, the predominant image is that of an eagle clutching a flag. A poem to "Mother" says, "There's a dear little house inviting / In a dear little place I know […]." The backing is a large scale floral cotton print. A pillow cover of this same design was printed with the words "National Guard" below the poem, but this one has no such designation. Mold is present on the back of the pillow cover and, unfortunately, it has come through to the front and shows in brownish stains behind the poem. This photographs well and we are happy to present it, although with the mold present, it has no intrinsic value. Below, a view of the back indicates that the textile must have been stunning when brand new. 15.75" x 15.625". 1930s. No resale value. *Courtesy of Lyell D. Henry.*

Even after the more severe treatment of dry-cleaning, involving chemicals, heat, and tumbling, discoloration from the parasite organisms still clings to the back of the pillow cover. They thoroughly infiltrated the fabric. Heat will deactivate mold, so the colony is no longer active, but take extreme care to protect your own health, if you choose to do that. These pathogens can cause disease in humans if inhaled. Use a mask, gloves, and a hepa-filter vacuum if attempting to vacuum visible mold growth.

Mold is truly the worst enemy of textiles, especially rayon ones. Rayon holds moisture more readily than cotton. The fibers "adsorb moisture" in scientific words, and rayon is hygroscopic (attracts and holds water) due to the cellulosic (plant) fibers that are present. This souvenir of Tijuana, Mexico, is beautiful, except for the mold that it holds. Please place any infested pillow cover in a polyethylene bag until you can consult with a professional conservator, if the item is one you would like to keep. Store any moldy items separate from the rest of your collection!

If a person looks closely, it is evident that xerophilic fungi have taken over the surface of this rayon U.S. Army Air Forces pillow cover from San Antonio, Texas. The purchase price for this item was $10.50, not counting shipping. Beware of online auctions! 16.875" x 17". Circa 1947. No resale value.

This rayon souvenir pillow from Tijuana, Mexico, must have been lovely in its day, before the ravages of mold took their toll. Large hand-painted roses grace the surface, along with an identical scene to one on a previous souvenir pillow cover of this type featured in this book. A "To My Wife" poem says, "A darling little wife / has made my dreams / come true ~ […]." 15.25" x 16.875". Circa early twentieth century. No resale value. *Courtesy of Lyell D. Henry.*

Here is yet another example of mildew on the surface of a textile. In spite of the organic problem with this pillow cover, it is wonderful that it was saved, at least long enough for us to photograph it, as it records the memory of the "Tennessee Maneuvers of 1941," a more obscure topic related to World War II.

This rayon pillow cover is from the Tennessee Maneuvers, 1943. It features a "Mother" poem: "No friend half so near to me / No comrades so true / No pal half so dear to me / Mother as you. / No love half so sweet to me / No heart half so fine / As the love and the heart of you / Mother o' Mine." The flag looks very unusual, in the way it is stylistically divided. Sadly, mildew clings to the surface. 15.75" x 16.625". 1943. The purchase price was $4.99, plus shipping. No resale value. Had I known of its condition, I would not have purchased it! Nonetheless, buying this item was a point of departure into learning about the U.S. Army's "Tennessee Maneuvers." Learn more at: http://www.rootsweb.ancestry.com/~tnsummer/tid1943.htm or http://www.campforest.com/tennessee_maneuvers.html.

This textile is covered with fungi. Some people call this condition "foxing." According to Mary-Lou Florian, the two most common types of fungi originate from plant deterioration and are airborne pathogens. They are called Altenaria and Cladosporium.[5] Fungi reproduces asexually, and will grow, particularly if there are residues of food, starch or other substances on the cloth. This infestation reminds me of xerophilic fungi. That type of organism leaves a residue of small brown spots, often seen on old ephemera. In this case, the growth covers the surface of the textile.

This Fort Hood pillow cover is covered with fungi (mold and mildew).

A large red and gray diagonal flocked banner announces "Camp Hood, Texas" in bold lettering on this old U.S. Army pillow cover. In the lower right corner is a familiar "Mother and Dad" poem: "No one knows but Mother and Dad / About the smiles and tears we've had […]." Even though this item, with a yellow fringe, is badly stained by mold, it is great to be able to photograph it for this book. It recalls a time before this U.S. Army base was renamed "Fort Hood." Their emblem was apparently a ferocious panther and the words, "Seek, Strike, Destroy." This item is infiltrated with mold and mildew. 15.5" x 15.5". 1942-1945. No resale value. *Courtesy of Lyell D. Henry.*

This pillow cover from Fort Slocum has the worst case of mold I have yet seen, so bad, in fact, that we simply discarded it right after taking these photos of both the front and back.

This rayon pillow cover is from Fort Slocum, New York, which is close to New Rochelle, New York. The words on it simply say, "God Bless America, Sweet Land of Liberty." The color has a medium magenta background. With severe damage from water and mildew, this textile was beyond trying to save. Nonetheless, seeing it gave us a chance to learn about Fort Slocum, where the military cadence "Sound off, one, two" was invented in 1944. During World War II, some training was provided there by the U.S. Army, which also used the base for administrative office space. No resale value. *Courtesy of Lyell D. Henry.*

This pillow cover shows signs of being subjected to a lot of moisture that has resulted in a severe case of mold, so bad, in fact, that we discarded the pillow cover after photographing it. A good rule of thumb is to keep moldy and mildewed items away from other textiles. If you decide to keep them, wrap them in tissue and place them within a zipped polyethylene bag.

One wonders how this pillow cover ever got into this crumpled condition, but actually, for its age, it would be fine, except for its faded surface. Evidently, the ink colors were not light fast and have faded over the years. This pillow cover is notable in its simplicity. It offers simply the name "Louisville, Kentucky" and the words to a "Mother" poem.

If we could only know the "back stories" about many of these old items, specifically, where they were stored, or how they were used, we would have a much better understanding of how their actual use, display, cleaning, or storage has affected them.

Framing, in general, is not a good choice for these period textiles, unless the work is done by a professional conservator. Once, I saw a World War I pillow cover for sale online with the high asking price of $150, plus almost $70s for shipping. The pillow cover appears to have been mounted on a non-archival, cardboard background that clearly shows a visible infestation of "foxing" (xerophilic fungi). This fungi "problem" will only get worse! This only shows that the seller does not realize that the condition of a piece is more important than its age. The framed pillow did not sell, even after two or three attempts.

~~~~~

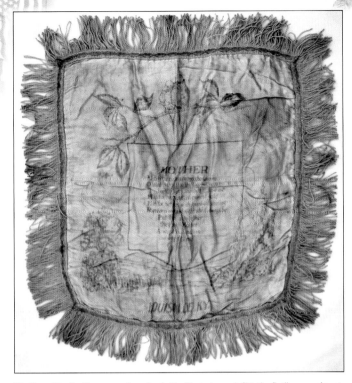

Motifs on this silk pillow cover from Louisville, Kentucky, early "Mother" pillow are almost indiscernible now. The fabric appears to be silk and the following poem is featured: "M is for the million things she gave me / O means only that she's growing old […]." At the top, there is a tree branch upon which sits two lovebirds, and trees and other foliage are depicted on the right and left bottom sides. This pillow cover seems to have suffered light damage with ultraviolet rays that altered the original, more vibrant hues. This textile has not been stored flat, which adds to a general look of disarray. 15.25" x 17". 1917-1918. The images have faded almost completely. No resale value. *Courtesy of Lyell D. Henry.*

In real estate, the repeated watch word is "location, location, location!" With textiles, it's "condition, condition, condition!" Some situations can be reversed with time and patience. A seam ripper is an indispensable tool in helping to remove lines of stitches previously sewn to close the pillow opening. Work from the "wrong side" and lift any hanging thread, gently tugging on it to loosen the stitch. Continue carefully, loosening and unpicking stitches, one by one. Usually the stitches are very tight and hard to dislodge, and often the stitches themselves have torn the fragile rayon fibers because the thread was stronger than the background fabric.

In some cases, the fringe has come loose, or the edges of the pillow have been so stretched, they have popped out. Often, the rayon threads have unraveled. If you really want to save the pillow so that it looks more presentable, there are several courses of action to take. Conceivably, one could take folded bias tape and enclose the damaged edge of rayon. Then one could reset the fringe. In that case, the pillow cover may become a little smaller than the original size.

Theoretically, one could fold over the damaged edge of the rayon, and then that edge could be serged with a serger to protect and enclose it, preparatory to sewing the fringe over it again. I have not tried that method and suspect that it would not be the ideal remedy.

In the case of old textiles, usually the best course of action is to take no action at all. World War I pillow covers, made of silk, are slowly disintegrating. Take care, even in moving them, making sure that you support them well with a piece of acid free, foam core board slipped underneath. All textiles have their own care requirements. As in the case of any textile, if you are unsure whether or not your planned intervention will be helpful, please consult a professional conservator in your area, especially if the item has some special meaning to you. To find a conservator near you, please visit this link: www.conservation-us.org.

This is but one example of rayon pillow covers that were sold after World War II as tourist souvenirs. This geographical souvenir textile celebrates Spooner, Wisconsin, and features images related to Native Americans. Until the 1960s, passenger trains ran to Spooner, "the "Crossroads of the North." It is a tourist location because of its "Railroad Memories Museum," "Wisconsin Canoe Heritage Museum," "Heart of the North Rodeo," and "Jack Pine Savage Days" Festival. The current population of this city, in which Highways 53 and 63, and 70 and 253 intersect, is 2,700 people. Travel seems to have become more widespread after World War II. 15.625" x 17.25". Circa 1960s. $5-10. *Courtesy of Lyell D. Henry.*

Chapter Ten

Generic Pillow Covers with Poems

Some pillow covers do not designate a specific branch of military service. Examples of some of these, that feature poems, are provided in this chapter.

This unusual "Sweetheart" pillow has a tag that says, "Spun Rayon 100%, Lining Rayon 100%, RN 37563, Made in Japan." It has a black background and the following words, "I love you when you're laughing, / I love you when you're sad, / [...]." The motifs appear to have been painted and most of the poem features metallic silver letters. A gate, two lovebirds, and roses are present and the poem is enclosed within a silver heart. Previously used, there is a small stain on the backing. The yellow fringe is .75" wide. 17.625" x 16.25". Post 1945. $20-25. *Courtesy of Lyell D. Henry.*

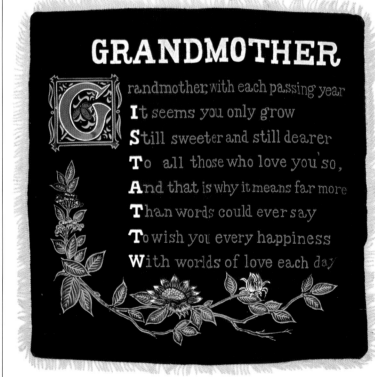

This pillow cover features a black spun rayon top and a rayon backing and is a rare "Grandmother" tribute. The words take up most of the design space and say, "Grandmother with each passing year / It seems you only grow / Still sweeter and still dearer / To all those who love you so. / And that is why it means far more / Than words could ever say / To wish you every happiness / With worlds of love each day." A tag states that this textile was "Made in Japan." The exceptionally short fringe is .375" wide. On the right side of the backing, there is an opening that closes with one snap. This item is showing some fold lines, but was never apparently used as a pillow. 16.75" x 16.75". Post-1945. $45-55. *Courtesy of Lyell D. Henry.*

This rayon, "Mother" pillow cover, with a light blue background, shows a woman sitting in a chair amid flowers. The poem is familiar by now, "M is for the million things she gave to me, / O means only that she's growing old. […]." The colors are "analogous" ones on the color wheel: green, blue, and purple, and the flowers have the appearance of being sketched and then filled in with color, although the design was surely printed. A variegated thread fringe completes the pillow. The backing is soft and in great condition; it feels like a thin felt. Considering the patina of the fabrics and the way in which the woman is attired, this appears to be an early twentieth century pillow cover. 16.625" x 16.75". Circa 1920s-1930s. $25-35. *Courtesy of Lyell D. Henry.*

A rayon "Mother" pillow features the same popular poem: "M is for the million things she gave to me, / O means only that she's growing old. […]." The background is white, and the poem is printed in large letters, in blue. There are four large, light red roses, two on either side of the poem, and a pink-orange fringe. Slightly stained on the front. The number "36" is sewn into the bottom edge of the front, on the inside. 15.75" x 16.5". 1941-1945. $20-25. *Courtesy of Lyell D. Henry.*

"Oh, the world is wide and the world is grand, / And there's a little or nothing new, / But the sweetest thing is the grip of the hand, / Of the Friend that's tried and true."
~ "Friend" pillow cover, Camp Carson, Colorado, U.S. Army

Poems from Additional Pillow Covers and Textiles

This study of Sweetheart and other souvenir and military collectible pillow covers has been an educational journey that has provided more insight for the author than anyone could have imagined! Besides the very graphic and colorful designs, the poetry found on pillow covers has a certain allure, even in its simplicity. For the record, I would like to share some additional lines of poetry seen on other pillow covers not in the author's collection. Most of the poems below were featured on World War II pillow covers. Others are seen on pillow pouches. Unless otherwise noted, the pillow covers mentioned are all from World War II.

Note that on the actual pillow covers incorrect spellings, grammar, capitalization or punctuation can be seen. In some cases, the actual presentation has been modified in order to keep the spell check function of the computer program happy.

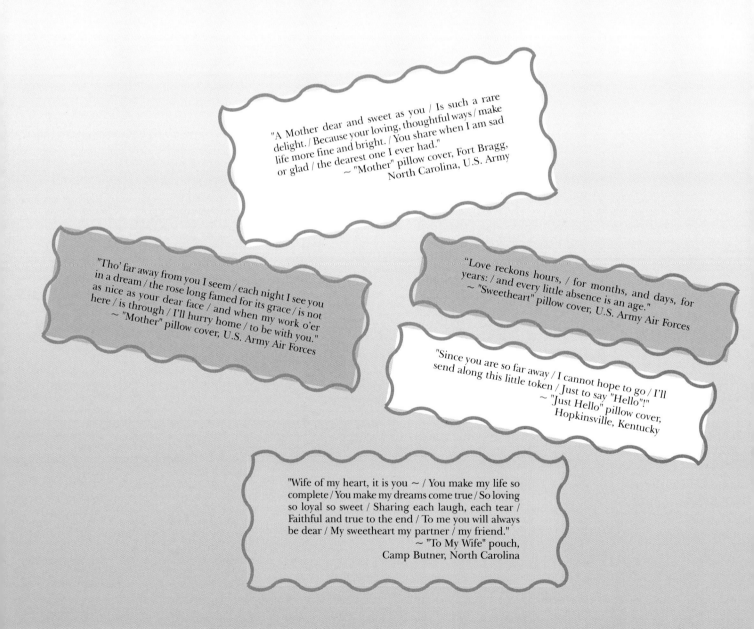

"A Mother dear and sweet as you / Is such a rare delight. / Because your loving, thoughtful ways / make life more fine and bright. / You share when I am sad or glad / the dearest one I ever had."
~ "Mother" pillow cover, Fort Bragg, North Carolina, U.S. Army

"Tho' far away from you I seem / each night I see you in a dream / the rose long famed for its grace / is not as nice as your dear face / and when my work o'er here / is through / I'll hurry home / to be with you."
~ "Mother" pillow cover, U.S. Army Air Forces

"Love reckons hours, / for months, and days, for years: / and every little absence is an age."
~ "Sweetheart" pillow cover, U.S. Army Air Forces

"Since you are so far away / I cannot hope to go / I'll send along this little token / Just to say "Hello"!"
~ "Just Hello" pillow cover, Hopkinsville, Kentucky

"Wife of my heart, it is you ~ / You make my life so complete / You make my dreams come true / So loving so loyal so sweet / Sharing each laugh, each tear / Faithful and true to the end / To me you will always be dear / My sweetheart my partner / my friend."
~ "To My Wife" pouch, Camp Butner, North Carolina

"I love your way / your laughter gay / each magic word / your dear lips say / I love your hands / your sweet commands / your heart that trusts / and understands / I love the sky above you." *(Mailed to Miss Connie Corella of Paterson, New Jersey, from Pvt. Joseph Dettorre during World War II.)*
~ "Sweetheart" pouch, Camp Lee, Virginia

"You're the very best couple that ever was paired / whatever was given alike you have shared / Many more years may your hearts be made glad / and may your blessings be many Dear Mother and Dad."
~ "Mother and Dad" pillow cover, Fort Sill, Oklahoma

"You came in my life –and then I learned / That dreams really can come true; / You came in my thoughts—and ever since / My thoughts are all of you; / You came in my heart and brought to me / The greatest joy I know; / And life is heaven on earth to me / Because I love you so."
~ "Sweetheart" pillow cover, Camp Davis, North Carolina, U.S. Army Camp Artillery Corps

This rayon pillow cover is unique due to its pastel background tints of pink and turquoise on a light pink background. The "Mother and Dad" poem says in large letters, "In all the years I've / known you both / You've planned and / strived for me [...]." Shown is a house in the country that has a chimney, and trees and land around it. A spray of *Rugosa Roses* extends up the left side and drapes over the top of the poem. This is very clean and was never used. 16.375" x 17". 1941-1945. $25-35. *Courtesy of Lyell D. Henry.*

"This Valentine will make it clear / That souls like yours / are forever dear." *(Miss Connie Corella, Paterson, New Jersey, received a rayon pillow cover from Pvt. Joseph Dettorre. With red and magenta background, red fringe, hearts, and roses.)*
~ "To My Valentine" pillow cover,
Camp Lee, Virginia, U.S. Armed Forces

"The beauty of a cultured pearl / Is likened to a certain girl / But lovely as the gem might be / There's none so rare as her to me / Her mem'ry is a thing apart ~ / A flawless image in my heart."
~ "To My Sweetheart" pillow cover,
Geneva, Nebraska, U.S. Army Air Forces

"I'm glad of the memories / of days you were near / Each memory I treasure / Each thought I hold dear / I remember each hour / I remember each day / You're always beside me / You're with me to stay."
~ "Remembrance" pillow cover, U.S. Army

"Thinking of our days together / and the things we say and do / Thinking of how very happy / I have been just loving you / A wish to you my darling / that will be my very best / Whispering "I love you truly" / more than you have guessed."
~ "Sweetheart" pillow cover,
Transfer, Pennsylvania, U.S. Army,
Shenanoo Personnel Replacement Poll

"I've gone to you / when things went wrong / and you've helped / and understood / When things went right / you shared my joys / and I'm happy / that you could / So I'm sending you / this gift of love / from across / the ocean blue / to tell you that I'm thankful / for a wonderful / Mother like you."
~ "Love to Mother" pillow cover, Hawaii
(military base and branch unknown)

"I love you for your kindly ways / your tender loving heart / your hands that since my / childhood days / have smoothed life's every smart / I love you for your cheery smile / through hours of cloud / or shine / for reasons new each little while / I love you / Mother mine."
~ "Mother Mine" pillow cover, U.S. Marines

"Nice to chat with / good to know; / glad to have her where I go, / Kind in trouble, bright in joy, / Suits exactly ~ can't say why, / Sweet and wholesome, always true, / That's my sister, yes, that's you."
~ "To My Sister" pillow cover, Camp Lee, Virginia

"As days pass by / never feel blue / for I remember the / happy times with you / it would lighten / my cares / and double my joys / to know that you / are remembering too."
~ "Remembering" pillow cover, Fort McClellan, Alabama

"I am grateful to heaven / for blessings it sent, / for peace and good fortune / for success and content, / I am grateful for help / for skies bright and blue, / But most grateful of all / for a Dad like you."
~ "Dad" pillow cover, Civilian Conservation Corps

Fort Crook, Omaha, Nebraska was established in 1918 and named for Major General George Crook (1828-1890), who fought in the Indian Wars and in the Civil War. The 61st Balloon Battalion was stationed at the site during World War I. However, in 1924, the decision was made to rename the site "Offutt Air Force Base," in honor of a World War I Pilot, First Lieutenant Jarvis Offutt (1894-1918), who died in France during the war. Offutt Air Force Base was the construction site of the first two bombers that dropped atomic bombs. Currently, the base is still in use.

"The Stars and Stripes Forever" is the theme of this rayon, patriotic, military pillow and has the poem, "Remembering." A large flag can be seen flying amid many planes in the "sky." The poem says, "It's nice to remember / with wishes for cheer. / someone like you / growing dearer each year [...]." A piece of masking tape used as a price tag has left residue on the surface. The tag said $3.00. 16.5" x 16.375". 1941-1945. $25-35. *Courtesy of Lyell D. Henry.*

The Stars and Stripes Forever

REMEMBERING

It's nice to remember
With wishes for cheer,
Someone like you
Growing dearer each year
It's nice to remember
Someone like you ~
But it's sweeter to know
You're remembering too.

OMAHA
NEBR.

"I'm thankful for a pal / Like you / So loyal and so fine / And I'll be grateful / All my life / That you sweetheart / Are mine!"
~ "My Wife" pillow cover, U.S. Army

"Did I ever tell you that / I love you. / Wife of mine indeed / I do. / I am fighting for you / and the U.S.A. / Remember this while / I'm away."
~ "Wife" pillow cover, Merchant Marine

"If I'd lost an angel / I couldn't have missed / her like I've missed you / my dearest sister."
~ "Sister" pillow cover, Camp Pendleton, U.S. Army

This rayon U.S. Army "Mother" pillow cover reminds one of Halloween with its orange flocked letters and Army insignia on a dark tan background. The poem says, "To one who bears the sweetest name / and adds a luster to the same [...]." This was never used. 16.25" x 17". 1941-1945. $10-15. *Courtesy of Lyell D. Henry*

"I never dreamed / I'd go thru life / with a girl like you / my darling wife."
~ "Dearest Wife" pillow cover, New Orleans, Louisiana, U.S. Army

"I miss your smile / your eyes that shine. / I love only you / sweetheart of mine."
~ "Sweetheart" pillow cover, Camp Haan, Riverside, California, U.S. Army

"Love reckons hours, for months, / and days, for years: / and every little absence / is an age."
~ Atlantic City, New Jersey, U.S. Army Air Forces

"Remembrance" is the theme of this rayon "Sister" pillow cover from the U.S. Army. The poem says, "Of all the girls / I ever knew / There never was / one like You […]." The color of the background is bright pink and the lettering and motifs are flocked in yellow. A tag sewn into a seam says, "Victory Emblem." The exact significance of those words is unknown. 15.875" x 17.625". 1945. $20-30. *Courtesy of Lyell D. Henry.*

This rayon pillow cover is for "Mother Dear," but has no designation of a military connection or geographical location. A poem is printed in navy blue on a light, blue-gray background. There is a navy blue fringe with yellow highlights. A shadow of purple runs behind the poem. Six roses and four rosebuds surround the poem, which says in large letters, all capitalized, "Six letters spell / the sweetest word / dearest ones I've ever heard. / In all the world / there is no other, / that means so much / as that word – Mother." This is a rarely seen poem. The pillow cover is in excellent condition. 15.75" x 17". 1941-1945. $20-25.

The coloration of the flocked images and words of this rayon pillow cover from World War I was irresistible! Basically, a red, white, and blue overall color scheme, the prominent words are "God Bless America" and "Liberty, Democracy, and Peace." A large eagle carrying a typical banner, "e *pluribus unum*," is the center decoration. The ivory background is tinted with patches of red and blue. The blue backing has some holes. 15.375" x 17.25". 1941-1945. $13-20.

"Its [sic] home that's best / the saying's surely true / For when my thoughts / would seek their rest, / They all come home to you."
~ "O East or West" pouch, U.S. Army, WWI

"I miss you sister I must / report; I realize now / you are a swell sport / We will win this war for / sisters like you / And be back / home 'ere you can say Boo."
~ "Sister" pillow cover, Fort Knox, Kentucky

A rayon pillow cover for Christmas was sent from New Orleans, Louisiana. A tank, a battleship, a plane, a candle, and sprigs of holly with bells accompany the words "Christmas Greetings" in green flocked letters. At the top of the pillow are the words "O'er The Land of the Free / And the Home of the Brave." 16.5" x 17.25". 1941-1945. $55-75.

"Then conquer we must, / For our cause it is just, / And this be our motto, ~ / In God is our trust."
~ "Victory" pillow cover, U.S. Navy

"This message is bringing / To far away YOU / A special "Hello" / And a warm "Howdy-do," / Some very glad mem'ries / Of what used to be / And many good wishes / From far away me!"
~ "Just Hello" pillow cover, Camp Barkeley, U.S. Army

"Just a few lines / yet you never could guess / How much love and good wishes / They're sent to express."
~ "Mother" pillow cover, U.S. Army

"Because of you there seems to be / just sunshine in the world for me. / I travel along life's sunny way with a song / in my heart that has come to stay. / Each task seems light and easy to do ~ / for your smile of courage helps me thru. / and life is glad and skies are blue / each day for me / because / of / you."
~ "To My Wife" pillow cover, camp and branch unknown

Chapter Eleven

Final Thoughts

This task of collecting pillow covers has been an extraordinary journey. A personal favorite of mine is this pillow that says, "Greetings from Alaska." The scene shows sled dogs, and that image calls to mind my aunt's husband, U.S. Army Master Sergeant Hendrik Dolleman (1905-1990). He immigrated to America from the Netherlands, and his U.S. Army buddies nicknamed him "Dutch." He accompanied Admiral Richard E. Byrd on two of his five expeditions to the Antarctic. Dolleman was responsible for training and managing sled dogs and their associated equipment.

He was involved in a much celebrated rescue mission in Greenland of a B-17 E bomber called, "My Gal Sal." While there have been many articles written about the rescue, you can read about it online at various sites, including: www.ultimatesacrifice. com/my_gal_sal_history.html. "Dolleman Island" is named in his honor, as noted in the book, *Antarctic Command* by Captain Finn Ronne, USNR.[1]

In reading about silk, rayon, and other cloth maps that guided pilots to safety if they were shot down, I collected a map that shows the island of Nantien in Southeast China where Captain Ted W. Lawson crashed his B-25 bomber. Initially, maps of this type were made of recycled parachute silk and often were printed on

This rayon pillow with heavily flocked motifs says, "Greetings from Alaska," and shows the Seal of the Territory of Alaska, which gained territorial status on August 24, 1912, and became our 49th state on January 3, 1959. The scene includes sled dogs, igloos, and the rising sun. The only other words present are "To My Wife." This pillow cover was a bit wrinkled from storage, but straightened out after the insertion of a pillow form. 16.5" x 16". 1912-1959. $20-30.

both sides. Later British escape maps were made of viscose rayon, or cuprammonium rayon, also known as Bemberg silk or copper rayon. Pilots carried them as part of a special waterproof pouch with a survival "kit" that contained money, a small brass compass, and a small hacksaw blade.[2] Kits were sold by the U.S. Army, the British, and the Australians during World War II. In addition, the government issued paper maps, but found that the cloth maps were more durable. Coveted by today's collectors, cloth maps in excellent condition are highly prized and more valued than others.

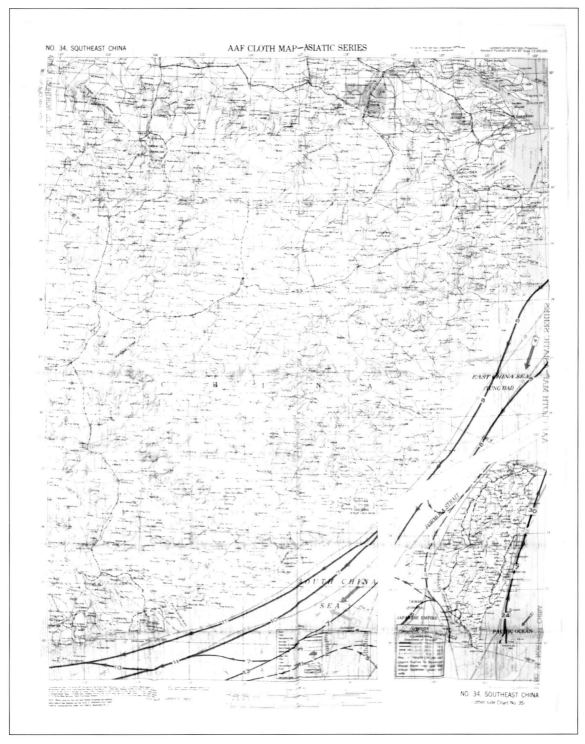

This is a double-sided cloth map printed by the U.S. Army. This is numbered 34 – Southeast China, on one side, and 35 – Northeast China, on the other side. The title of the map is "AAF Cloth Map: Asiatic Series." These maps were part of the "Escape and Evasion Survival Kits." 25.5" x 20.5". 1944. $45-50.

If one word could be chosen to describe the purpose of most of the textiles featured in this book, the word might be "Remembrance." As we have seen, they all served a mnemonic purpose: some commemorate events, such as the "Punitive Expedition" and others honor military or political leaders of the day, such as Pershing or Clemenceau (during World War I). Still other textiles were intended to be souvenirs from specific military bases or tourist locations. The bulk of the pillow covers shown here offer a sentimental tribute to a specific loved one.

While one pillow cover could seem inconsequential to the unknowing, in viewing all of them as a class of material objects, a person can begin to understand their importance to people who exchanged them during the first half of the twentieth century.

With their bright colors and touching graphics, they could bolster the spirits of both the giver and the receiver, just as we feel happy in seeing them again today. Although, the "back story" of the circumstances in which each pillow cover was presented may be lost to history, perhaps that is just part of their mystery and charm. My life is all the richer for the experience of researching and writing about these collectible textiles. Long overlooked, they have stood the test of time and are with us still.

Patches are another category of military collectibles. After seeing this Polar bear patch, printed on a pillow cover with the name of Fort Richardson, Alaska, I added this patch to my collection. As stated in a photo caption that appears in Chapter Four, the patch represents Alaska's Department of the Army. Just as one road leads onto another, I purchased a black cat patch that is the symbol of the 81st Infantry Division in both World War I and World War II. The "wildcat" was mentioned previously, at the beginning of the book and in chapter four. We have come full circle.

All of these pillow covers bring back a time, a place, an event. Some history that was not recorded has been lost. For me, the study and research involved in preparing this book has provided more insights and discoveries than I could have imagined. This most enjoyable journey was made much easier because of the Internet. Online vendors gave me the opportunity to add more textile examples to my collection.

Many colorful pillow covers have been presented here, with strong graphics, and only barely imagined personal meaning. They represent many specific military bases and demonstrate the pride that men and women embraced in being members of the branches of service represented here. There seems to be no limit to the types of organizations honored by these humble textiles. Recently, there was a pillow cover offered for West Point; and others for India and Burma, countries we hardly think of when now recalling the events of World War II. We are forever indebted to those who diligently saved all of these textile treasures that continue to have meaning today for those who appreciate them! Happy collecting!

This small round patch with the head of a Polar Bear was issued by the Alaska Department of the U.S. Army. It represents Alaska Territory and is from the World War II era. The diameter measures 2.625". 1941-1945. $15-20.

This black "wildcat" was previously mentioned in the introduction to this book in reference to a World War I pillow cover that said, "Treat 'em Rough." This patch is from World War II and symbolizes the 81st U.S. Army Infantry Division. The diameter of the badge measures 2.25". 1941-1945. $10-15.

Endnotes

Chapter Two

1. Paul S. Boyer, ed., *The Oxford Companion to United States History*, 589.
2. *Ibid*.
3. http://en.wikipedia.org/wiki/John_J_Pershing, 10.
4. http://en.wikipedia.org/wiki/Pancho_Villa_Expedition.
5. http://www.military-historians.org/company/chapters/wpabsent.htm.
6. http://en.wikipedia/wiki/Camp_Cody
7. http://en.wikipedia.org/wiki/Nathan_Bedford_Forrest.
8. David P. Smith, "World War I Pagers – Terms." AAC World History Message Board. America Online (Electronic Communication Network). Vienna, VA: AOL, 1996.
9. http://www.oldmagazinearticles.com/pdf/doughboy_word_origin.pdf
10. http://www.worldwar1.com/dbc/origindb.html.
11. http://en.wikipedia.org/wiki/Georges_Clemenceau, 2.
12. http://en.wikipedia.org/wiki/Georges_Clemenceau.
13. http://en.wikipedia.org/wiki/Georges_Clemenceau, 7.
14. John J. Pershing, *My Experiences in the World War: Volume 11*, 397.
15. http://www.mccoy.army.mil/FactsSheets/index.asp?id=wwii.
16. http://en.wikipedia.org/wiki/Fort_McCoy_Wisconsin.
17. http://www.history.navy.mil/photos/sh-usn/usnsh-1/id1326.htm

Chapter Three

1. David D. Draves, *Builders of Men: Life in C.C.C. Camps of New Hampshire*, 268.

2. *Ibid*.
3. http://tinyurl.com/37ykk6y

Chapter Four

1. Sara J. Kadolph and Anna L. Langford, *Textiles, Ninth Edition*, 80.
2. http://en.wikipedia.org/wiki/Fort_Sill.
3. http://en.wikipedia.org/wiki/Fort_Benning.
4. http://en.wikipedia.org/wiki/William_Pitt,_1st_Earl_of_Chatham.
5. http://en.wikipedia.org/wiki/99th_Infantry_Division_(United_States).
6. *Ibid*.
7. http://en.wikipedia.org/wiki/Fort_Stewart.
8. http://en.wikipedia.org/wiki/Fort_Bragg_(North_Carolina).
9. http://en.wikipedia.org/wiki/Fort_Belvoir.
10. http://en.wikipedia.org/wiki/Fort_Hood.
11. http://en.wikipedia.org/wiki/Camp_Wheeler.
12. http://en.wikipedia.org/wiki/Nancy_Lincoln.
13. http://en.wikipedia.org/wiki/Camp_Blanding.
14. http://en.wikipedia.org/wiki/Camp_Maxey.
15. http://www.history.army.mil/books/cg&csa/wood-1.html.
16. http://en.wikipedia.org/wiki/Fort_Leonard_Wood_(military_base).
17. http://en.wikipedia.org/wiki/Camp_Stoneman.
18. http://www.johnbellhood.org/bio-06.htm.
19. http://en.wikipedia.org/wiki/Joseph_Gilbert_Totten.

20. http://en.wikipedia.org/wiki/Fort_ Totten_(New_York).

21. http://en.wikipedia.org/wiki/Fort_ Monmouth.

22. http://www.britannica.com/EBchecked/ topic/371456/George-G-Meade.

23. http://en.wikipedia.org/wiki/Fort_ George_G_Meade.

24. http://en.wikipedia.org/wiki/Camp_ Atterbury.

25. Kadolph and Langford, 490.

26. http://www.militarymuseum.org/ CpKohler.html.

27. http://www.schistory.net/campcroft/ history.html.

28. http://en.wikipedia.org/wiki/Camp_ Livingston.

29. http://en.wikipedia.org/wiki/Fort_Dix.

30. http://en.wikipedia.org/wiki/Marine_ Corps_Outlying_Field_Camp_Davis.

31. http://en.wikipedia.org/wiki/George_ Armstrong_Custer.

32. http://en.wikipedia.org/wiki/Fort_ Custer_Training_Center.

33. http://en.wikipedia.org/wiki/Wilds_P._ Richardson.

34. http://en.wikipedia.org/wiki/Fort_ Richardson.

35. http://www.parsons.com/projects/Pages/ camp-sibert-site-8.aspx.

36. http://www.fortdevensmuseum.org/ FirstDevensHospital.html.

37. http://www.fortdevensmuseum.org/ history.html.

38. http://en.wikipedia.org/wiki/Camp_ Bowie.

39. http://en.wikipedia.org/wiki/Camp_ Kilmer.

40. http://en.wikipedia.org/wiki/Fort_ Knox.

41. http://en.wikipedia.org/wiki/Fort_ Riley.

42. *Op.cit.*

43. http://www.mybaseguide.com/army/ fort-knox/armor-center.aspx.

44. http://tennesseeencyclopedia.net/ imagegallery.php?EntryID=C012.

45. *Ibid.*

46. http://en.wikipedia.org/wiki/Camp_ Mackall.

47. http://en.wikipedia.org/wiki/Fort_ Bliss.

48. http://en.wikipedia.org/William_ Wallace_Smith_Bliss.

49. http://en.wikipedia.org/wiki/Camp_ Shelby.

50. Ibid, 2.

51. http://en.wikipedia/org/wiki/Camp_ Pickett.

52. http://en.wikipedia/org/wiki/ Occupation_of_Japan.

53. http://en.wikipedia/org/wiki/Fort_ Snelling_Minnesota.

54. Ibid.

55. Richard E. Osborne, *World War II Sites in the United States: A Tour Guide & Directory*, 151.

56. http://en.wikipedia.org/wiki/Camp_ Ashland.

57. http://en.wikipedia.org/wiki/ William_C.C._Claiborne.

58. http://en.wikipedia.org/wiki/Camp_ Claiborne.

59. http://en.wikipedia.org/wiki/Winfield_ Scott.

60. http://www.militarymuseum.org/ FtScott.html.

61. Osborne, 11-12.

62. *Ibid*, 135.

63. http://www.militarymuseum.org/ RobertsCMH.html.

64. http://www.militarymuseum.org/ campbob.html.

65. http://en.wikipedia.org/wiki/Fort_ Jackson_(South_Carolina)

66. Osborne, 226.

67. http://en.wikipedia.org/wiki/Camp_ Barkeley.

68. http://en.wikipedia.org/wiki/Camp_ Rucker.

69. Osborne, 3.

70. http://en.wikipedia.org/wiki/Camp_ Shelby.

Chapter Five

1. http://en.wikipedia.org/wiki/United_ States_Army_Air_Forces.

2. http://en.wikipedia.org/wiki/Seymour_ Johnson_Air_Force_Base.

3. http://en.wikipedia.org/wiki/McClellan_ Air_Force_Base.

4. http://en.wikipedia.org/wiki/Air_ Training_Command.

5. http://en.wikipedia.org/wiki/Buckley_ Air_Force_Base.

6. http://www.nytimes.com/1993/09/28/obituaries/james-doolittle-96-pioneer-aviator-who-led-first-raid-on-japan-dies.html.

7. http://www.hmbd.org/marker.asp?marker=10680.

8. http://en.wikipedia.org/wiki/Lackland_Air_Force_Base.

9. http://Tampa_International_Airport.

10. http://www.fsu.edu/~ww2/fl_during_ww2/florida_military_bases.htm.

11. Osborne, 275.

12. http://www.consolidatedaircraft.org/rhf.html.

13. *Ibid*.

14. http://en.wikipedia.org/wiki/Scott_Air_Force_Base.

15. Osborne, 72.

16. *Ibid*, 72.

17. http://www.kirtland.af.mil/library/factsheets/factsheetasp?id=5301.

18. http://en.wikipedia.org/wiki/Kirtland_Air_Force_Base.

19. http://www.wallawallaairport.com/ownership/history.cfm.

20. Osborne, 236.

Chapter Six

1. http://en.wikipedia.org/wild/Seabee.

2. Ibid.

3. http://en.wikipedia.org/wiki/Juan_Rodríguez_Cabrillo.

4. http://en.wikipedia.org/wiki/.

5. Op.cit.

6. http://www.usswestvirginia.org/us_west_virginia_history.htm.

7. http://en.wikipedia.org/wiki/Naval/Submarine_Base_New_London.

8. Osborne, 78.

9. http://en.wikipedia.org/wiki/United_States_Naval_Training_Center_Bainbridge.

10. http://en.wikipedia.org/wiki/Kaiser_Shipyards.

11. Doris Kearns Goodwin, *No Ordinary Time: Franklin & Eleanor Roosevelt: The Home Front in World War II*, Caption #8, second set of photo inserts.

Chapter Seven

1. James Warren, *American Spartans, The U.S. Marines: A Combat History from Iwo Jima to Iraq*, (no page cited in online source).

2. James Bradley, *Flags of Our Fathers*, 410.

3. Richard Tregaskis, *Guadalcanal Diary*, 29 & 173.

4. http://en.wikipedia.org/wiki/Raising_the_Flag_on_Iwo_Jima, 8.

5. Bradley, 210.

6. http://www.hmdb.org/marker.asp?marker=2794.

7. http://en.wikipedia.org/wiki/United_States_Maritime_Service.

8. http://en.wikipedia.org/wiki/Santa_Catalina_Island_California.

9. http://www.dvrbs.com/monuments/camden/camden.nj-ww2-merchant-marine-memorial.htm.

10. http://flightpundit.com/archives/206/06/23/acta-non-verba/.

Chapter Nine

1. George E. Linton, Ph.D., TexScD, *The Modern Textile and Apparel Dictionary, 4th edition*, 461.

2. Information from Mary-Lou Florian, mycologist, on November 17, 2010, via e-mail.

3. *Op.cit*, 3.

4. Conversation with Dr. Margaret T. Ordoñez at the University of Rhode Island on October 13, 2010.

5. Information from Mary-Lou Florian, mycologist, on November 17, 2010, via e-mail.

Chapter Eleven

1. Ronne, 221.

2. http://www.escapemaps.com/history_of_wwii_british_cloth_escape_maps.htm#A.___MI_9_and_Clayton_Hutton.

Bibliography

Boyer, Paul S., editor. *The Oxford Companion to United States History*. Oxford, New York and other locations: Oxford University Press, 2001.

Bradley, James. *Flags of Our Fathers*. New York, New York: Bantam Books, 2006.

Chase, Joseph Cummings. *Face Value: Autobiography of the Portrait Painter*. New York, New York: Rolton House, Inc., 1962.

Draves, David D. *Builder of Men: Life in C.C.C. Camps of New Hampshire*. Portsmouth, New Hampshire: Peter E. Randall, Publisher, 1992.

Goodwin, Doris Kearns. *No Ordinary Time: Franklin & Eleanor Roosevelt: The Home Front in World War II*. New York, New York: Simon and Schuster Paperbacks, 1994.

Henderson, Kristin. *While They're at War: The True Story of American Families on the Homefront*. Boston and New York: Houghton Mifflin Company, 2006.

Kadolph, Sara J. and Anna L. Langford, *Textiles, Ninth Edition*. Langford, New Jersey: Pearson Education, Inc., 2002.

Lawson, Captain Ted W. *Thirty Seconds Over Tokyo*. New York, New York: Random House, Inc., 1943.

Linton, Ph.D., TexScD, George E. *The Modern Textile and Apparel Dictionary, 4th edition*. Ann Arbor, Michigan: Braum, Brumfield, Inc., 1973.

Osborne, Richard E. *World War Sites In The United States: A Tour Guide & Directory*. Indianapolis, Indiana: Riebel-Roque Publishing Co., 1998.

Perry, John. *Sgt. York: His Life, Legend, & Legacy*. Nashville, Tennessee: B & H Publishing Group, 1997.

Pershing, John J. *My Experiences in the World War, Volume I and Volume 2*. New York, New York: Frederick A. Stokes Company, MCMXXXI (1931).

Ronne, USNR, Captain Finn, *Antarctic Command*. Indianapolis, Indiana and New York, New York: Bobbs-Merrill Company, 1961.

Tregaskis, Richard. *Guadalcanal Diary*. New York, New York: Random House, 1955.

Warren, James. *American Spartans, The U.S. Marines: A Combat History from Iwo Jima to Iraq*. New York, New York: Free Press, Simon & Schuster, 2005.

Wylie, Philip. *A Generation of Vipers*. New York, New York: Rinehart, 1942.

Index